Microservices with Java: Build Scalable and Flexible Applications

A Step-by-Step Guide to Developing Microservices with Java

BOOZMAN RICHARD

BOOKER BLUNT

All rights reserved

Table of Content

TABLE OF CONTENTS

INTRODUCTION 7

Microservices with Java build and Flexible Applications: ..7

Why This Book Is Essential..8

What You Will Learn 9

Who This Book Is For...11

Why React, Angular, and Vue.js? 12

Conclusion 13

Chapter 1 14

Introduction to Microservices Architecture 14

Summary: 20

Chapter 2 21

The Evolution of Software Architecture............................21

Summary: 29

Chapter 3 30

Core Concepts in Microservices 30

Summary: 39

Chapter 4 40

Setting Up Your Development Environment......................40

Summary: 49

Chapter 5 51

Building Your First Microservice with Java and Spring Boot...51

Summary: 60

Chapter 6 61

Service Communication in Microservices 61

    Summary: 71

Chapter 7 73

Securing Microservices with OAuth2 and JWT 73

    Summary: 83

Chapter 8 85

Managing Microservices with Spring Cloud 85

    Summary: 94

Chapter 9 96

Database Integration in Microservices 96

    Summary 106

Chapter 10 108

Asynchronous Messaging with Kafka 108

    Summary 118

Chapter 11 119

Service Discovery and Load Balancing 119

    Summary 129

Chapter 12 130

Microservices Resilience with Hystrix 130

    Summary 139

Chapter 13 140

Deploying Microservices with Docker 140

    Summary 148

Chapter 14 150

Kubernetes: Orchestrating Microservices at Scale 150

    Summary 159

Chapter 15 161

CI/CD for Microservices with Jenkins.................................161

    Summary 170

Chapter 16...172

Monitoring and Logging in Microservices 172

    Summary 182

Chapter 17...184

Testing Microservices..184

    Summary 195

Chapter 18...197

Handling Distributed Transactions 197

    Summary 207

Chapter 19...209

Event-Driven Microservices 209

    Summary 220

Chapter 20...221

API Gateway and Gateway Offloading 221

    Summary 232

Chapter 21...233

Security Best Practices for Microservices 233

    Summary 241

Chapter 22...243

Microservices with Serverless Architectures.........................243

    Summary 253

Chapter 23...255

Optimizing Microservices Performance 255

    Summary 264

Chapter 24...266

Scaling Microservices..266

INTRODUCTION

Microservices with Java build and Flexible Applications:

The web development landscape has evolved dramatically over the past decade, with JavaScript frameworks playing a pivotal role in shaping how developers build interactive, dynamic, and scalable applications. In this rapidly changing ecosystem, staying up to date with the latest frameworks and technologies is crucial to building high-performance web applications that meet user expectations for speed, reliability, and seamless experiences across devices.

This book, *Mastering JavaScript Frameworks: From React to Angular*, is designed to be your comprehensive guide to mastering the most popular JavaScript frameworks used in modern web development. Whether you are just starting your journey into web development or you're a seasoned developer looking to deepen your knowledge, this book covers everything you need to know about **React**, **Angular**, and **Vue.js**. Each chapter is crafted to provide you with a clear understanding of the core concepts, best practices, and real-world examples, helping you build scalable, maintainable, and performant applications.

Why This Book Is Essential

The demand for rich, interactive web applications has never been higher. With the rise of Single Page Applications (SPAs), Progressive Web Apps (PWAs), and mobile-first design, developers must not only understand the principles of front-end development but also leverage modern JavaScript frameworks to enhance the user experience and meet the growing demands of today's digital world.

In this book, you will:

- Gain a deep understanding of **React**, **Angular**, and **Vue.js**, each of which has its unique strengths and weaknesses.
- Learn how to implement best practices for building fast, efficient, and secure web applications.
- Dive into advanced topics such as **state management**, **routing**, **service workers**, and **performance optimization**.
- Explore real-world examples of building web apps from scratch, including integrating APIs, securing user data, and optimizing performance.

- Get hands-on experience with building **Progressive Web Apps (PWAs)**, **Single Page Applications (SPAs)**, and mobile-first web solutions.

Whether you're looking to improve your skills in building scalable front-end applications or need to stay updated with the latest trends and technologies in web development, this book will serve as your essential companion.

What You Will Learn

In the first part of the book, we'll explore the foundational concepts of JavaScript frameworks. You'll get acquainted with the core principles behind **React**, **Angular**, and **Vue.js**, including their strengths, weaknesses, and appropriate use cases. We'll dive into the fundamentals of each framework, helping you choose the right tool for your next project.

Next, we will cover how to build real-world applications with these frameworks. You'll learn how to develop powerful web apps by creating dynamic user interfaces, managing state effectively, and implementing modern features like **routing**, **authentication**, and **data binding**. You'll also get hands-on experience building **single-page**

applications (SPAs) and integrating APIs to enhance the functionality of your app.

As we move deeper into advanced topics, the book will guide you through **state management** using libraries like **Redux** for React, **NgRx** for Angular, and **Vuex** for Vue.js. We'll also focus on performance optimization techniques such as **code splitting**, **lazy loading**, **caching**, and **progressive web apps (PWAs)** to ensure that your web apps perform at their best across all devices and network conditions.

Security is also a major concern when developing web applications. In this book, we'll explore how to protect your app from common vulnerabilities like **Cross-Site Scripting (XSS)**, **Cross-Site Request Forgery (CSRF)**, and **SQL Injection**. You'll learn how to implement secure authentication systems using **JWT** (JSON Web Tokens) and other modern techniques to safeguard your app's data and user privacy.

The final section of the book covers best practices and strategies for maintaining and evolving your web apps. We'll focus on **test-driven development (TDD)**, **unit testing**, and **end-to-end testing** with tools like **Jest**, **Karma**, and **Protractor**. We'll also discuss how to stay up to date with the latest trends and frameworks in the JavaScript ecosystem, ensuring your skills remain relevant in the ever-changing world of web development.

Who This Book Is For

This book is intended for developers of all experience levels who want to master modern JavaScript frameworks. Whether you are:

- A **beginner** looking to get started with React, Angular, or Vue.js, and want to learn the fundamentals of web development with modern frameworks.
- An **intermediate developer** who wants to deepen your understanding of state management, routing, testing, and performance optimization.
- An **experienced developer** seeking to stay updated on the latest tools, best practices, and trends in JavaScript frameworks, and how to build scalable, secure, and high-performance web applications.

Why React, Angular, and Vue.js?

The three frameworks covered in this book—**React**, **Angular**, and **Vue.js**—are the most widely used and popular choices for building web applications today. Each framework has unique features, and understanding their strengths and use cases will help you choose the right one for your project.

- **React**: Known for its simplicity and flexibility, React is a **JavaScript library** for building user interfaces. Its component-based architecture and virtual DOM make it highly efficient for rendering dynamic UIs, and it is widely adopted for creating modern, fast web applications.
- **Angular**: Angular is a **full-fledged framework** that provides everything you need for building large-scale web applications. With built-in tools like **dependency injection**, **routing**, and **forms management**, Angular is perfect for building complex, enterprise-level apps.
- **Vue.js**: Vue is a **progressive framework** that is both easy to learn and flexible enough to scale for large applications. It combines the best features of both React and Angular, offering an approachable

learning curve with powerful tools for building dynamic, modern web apps.

By the end of this book, you'll have a solid understanding of these frameworks and the ability to build robust, production-ready web apps with them.

Conclusion

The world of JavaScript frameworks is constantly evolving, and staying up-to-date with the latest tools and techniques is essential for becoming a proficient web developer. *Mastering JavaScript Frameworks: From React to Angular* offers a detailed, hands-on guide to building modern web applications that are fast, scalable, and secure. By mastering these frameworks, you'll be equipped to tackle any web development challenge and stay at the forefront of the ever-changing landscape of web technologies.

Whether you're building a personal project or working on an enterprise-level application, the skills and knowledge you gain from this book will serve as a solid foundation for your future web development career. Let's dive in and explore the power of **React**, **Angular**, and **Vue.js**, and start building modern web apps that users love!

CHAPTER 1

INTRODUCTION TO MICROSERVICES ARCHITECTURE

What are Microservices?

Microservices is an architectural style that structures an application as a collection of loosely coupled, independently deployable services. Each service is small, self-contained, and focused on doing a specific task or business function. Rather than building an entire system as a single, monolithic application, microservices break down complex systems into smaller, more manageable pieces.

Each microservice operates in its own process and communicates with other services via lightweight mechanisms, typically HTTP or message queues, using well-defined APIs (often RESTful or GraphQL). Microservices are built around business capabilities and can be developed, deployed, and scaled independently. This approach helps teams to work autonomously and allows for better management of complex systems.

Traditional Monolithic Applications vs. Microservices

Monolithic Applications:

- A monolithic application is typically built as a single, unified codebase where all the components (user interface, database access, business logic, etc.) are tightly integrated and packaged into one executable unit.
- The entire application needs to be deployed as a single unit, even for minor changes. This can lead to slower release cycles and difficulty in scaling specific components.
- In monolithic systems, the failure of one part of the application could potentially bring down the entire system.
- Example: Traditional e-commerce applications or legacy systems where the front-end, business logic, and database logic all reside within a single unit.

Microservices:

- Microservices split an application into a collection of small services that each perform a distinct function. For example, a payment service, an inventory service, and a shipping service.

- Each service is independently deployable and can be scaled individually, providing flexibility for both deployment and scaling.

- Failures in one service do not affect the entire system, since the services are loosely coupled and operate independently. This increases resilience and fault tolerance.

- Communication between microservices is usually done via lightweight protocols like HTTP, REST, or messaging queues.

- Example: An e-commerce platform where payment processing, inventory management, and customer authentication are handled by separate microservices.

Benefits of Microservices: Scalability, Flexibility, Fault Isolation

1. Scalability:

- One of the biggest advantages of microservices is the ability to scale individual components of an application independently. If one service experiences a high load, it can be scaled up (by deploying additional instances) without affecting the rest of the system.

- For example, if an e-commerce platform's payment service is receiving higher traffic during sales events, that specific service can be scaled independently while other services, like the user authentication service, can remain on a smaller scale.

2. Flexibility:

- Microservices offer flexibility in terms of technology and development processes. Different teams can use different technologies for different services. For instance, the inventory management service might be built using Java, while the customer authentication service could be written in Python, and both can work together seamlessly.
- It also allows teams to adopt new technologies without having to refactor the entire system. If one microservice becomes outdated or less efficient, it can be replaced with a better solution without disrupting other services.

3. Fault Isolation:

- Microservices architecture offers inherent fault isolation. If one microservice fails, the rest of the system can continue functioning without being affected.
- For example, in a shopping cart system, if the payment processing service goes down, customers can still browse products and add items to their cart, and the failure won't impact the product recommendation or user account services.

- Fault isolation is key for building resilient systems, as failures are easier to manage and contain without causing cascading issues.

Real-World Examples of Companies Using Microservices

1. Netflix:

- Netflix is one of the most widely recognized examples of microservices in action. Initially, Netflix used a monolithic architecture, but as it grew, they needed a more scalable solution to handle its vast global user base. Netflix transitioned to a microservices architecture, where different services such as content delivery, user recommendations, payment processing, and content management are all handled by separate microservices.
- This change allowed Netflix to scale individual services, improve fault tolerance, and deploy new features quickly without affecting the overall user experience.

2. Uber:

- Uber is another company that uses microservices to power its platform. The Uber system has thousands of microservices that handle everything from ride matching to payment processing and driver management.
- For example, Uber's ride-matching service runs independently of its payment service, meaning that if

18

there's an issue with payment processing, riders and drivers can still interact via the ride-matching service.

- By using microservices, Uber can scale the system as demand grows, particularly during peak hours, and isolate failures to ensure the user experience remains intact.

3. Amazon:

- Amazon also adopted microservices early on to break down its complex e-commerce platform into small, independently deployable services. From inventory management to order processing and customer recommendations, each component is handled by a separate service.

- This architecture has allowed Amazon to scale its systems effectively while introducing new features and services without interrupting the overall platform.

4. Spotify:

- Spotify, the music streaming giant, also utilizes a microservices-based architecture to handle its music delivery, user recommendations, playlists, and user accounts. Each feature is implemented as a set of independent microservices, making it easier to innovate and deploy new features without disrupting the system.

- Their architecture allows them to handle millions of users, each with unique preferences, without compromising on performance or reliability.

Summary:

In this chapter, we've explored the fundamentals of microservices architecture. Microservices provide a flexible, scalable, and fault-tolerant approach to building complex applications by dividing them into small, independent services. This contrasts with traditional monolithic applications, which are tightly coupled and more difficult to scale or modify. We've also looked at some real-world examples, including Netflix, Uber, Amazon, and Spotify, to illustrate how leading companies use microservices to enhance their systems' flexibility and scalability.

As we proceed through the book, you will learn how to design, develop, and deploy microservices using Java, focusing on building systems that are robust, easy to maintain, and scalable.

CHAPTER 2

THE EVOLUTION OF SOFTWARE ARCHITECTURE

Historical Context: Monolithic, SOA (Service-Oriented Architecture)

1. Monolithic Architecture: Monolithic architecture refers to a traditional software design where all components of an application are combined into a single, unified codebase. A monolithic application typically includes the user interface (UI), business logic, and database access within the same system. This unified design was the standard for many years and is still used today in many legacy systems.

Challenges of Monolithic Architecture:

- **Tightly Coupled:** All parts of the application are interdependent. A change in one part often requires changes to other parts, making the system rigid and difficult to maintain.

- **Scalability Issues:** Scaling a monolithic system can be inefficient. Since the entire application is treated as a single unit, scaling it often means replicating the whole system rather than individual components. This can lead to resource wastage.

- **Long Deployment Cycles:** Any updates or new features require redeploying the entire application. As systems grow in complexity, the time taken for deployment increases, leading to slower release cycles.

- **Difficult to Innovate:** With monolithic systems, adopting new technologies or making architectural changes requires significant effort and a complete overhaul of the entire application.

Real-World Example of Monolithic Systems:

- A traditional e-commerce platform built as a monolithic application could have a single codebase handling everything: product listings, order processing, user authentication, and payment management. If any part of the system needs to be updated, the whole application must be redeployed, leading to downtime and coordination challenges.

2. Service-Oriented Architecture (SOA): Service-Oriented Architecture (SOA) emerged as a response to the challenges of monolithic systems. SOA encourages designing an application as a collection of loosely coupled, reusable services that communicate over a network, typically using standardized protocols like SOAP (Simple Object Access Protocol) or HTTP.

Key Features of SOA:

- **Loose Coupling:** Each service operates independently and interacts with other services through well-defined interfaces.
- **Reusability:** Services are designed to be reusable across different systems or applications.
- **Interoperability:** Services can interact with each other, even if they are built using different technologies, thanks to standardized communication protocols.
- **Centralized Governance:** SOA often relies on a central service bus or middleware to manage communication, ensuring coordination across services.

Challenges of SOA:

- **Complexity:** While SOA offers more flexibility than monolithic systems, it can become complex in terms of service management, orchestration, and monitoring. Each service requires careful design and integration.
- **Overhead:** SOA typically relies on heavier protocols like SOAP, which can introduce performance overhead.
- **Centralized Control:** While services are loosely coupled, managing and maintaining the architecture often requires centralized control, leading to potential bottlenecks.

Real-World Example of SOA:

- A large organization, like a bank, may use SOA to manage various services such as customer authentication, transaction processing, and loan approvals. These services communicate over a service bus and are designed to work independently of one another.

How Microservices Fit into the Evolution of Software Design

Microservices emerged as a natural evolution of SOA, building on the concept of breaking down applications into smaller, independent services. However, unlike SOA, which often relies on centralized governance and complex communication mechanisms, microservices embrace a decentralized approach, aiming to provide greater flexibility, scalability, and autonomy.

Key Differences Between Microservices and SOA:

- **Decentralization:** While SOA relies on a central service bus or middleware to manage communication, microservices take a decentralized approach, with each service managing its own logic, data, and communication patterns. Each service operates independently, without the need for a central coordination mechanism.
- **Technology Heterogeneity:** Microservices embrace technology diversity. Each microservice can be developed using different programming languages,

databases, and tools, based on the specific requirements of the service. This is in contrast to SOA, where services often need to use similar technologies for easy integration.

- **Granularity:** Microservices focus on smaller, more focused services. Each microservice is designed to handle a specific business capability, with well-defined boundaries. In comparison, SOA services tend to be larger and may encompass multiple business capabilities.

- **Communication:** While SOA services often communicate using heavyweight protocols like SOAP, microservices typically use lightweight, faster protocols like HTTP or message queues (e.g., Kafka, RabbitMQ) for communication.

In essence, microservices build upon the foundational ideas of SOA but take them further by promoting a truly decentralized, autonomous architecture that is more suited for modern, agile development practices.

Key Drivers for the Shift to Microservices

The shift from monolithic systems and SOA to microservices has been driven by several factors, including the need for scalability, flexibility, and agility in modern software development. Let's explore some of the main drivers:

25

1. Scalability and Elasticity:

- **Scaling Individual Components:** Microservices allow for scaling individual services independently based on demand. This is much more efficient than scaling a monolithic application, where scaling requires replicating the entire system.

- **Elastic Scaling:** With cloud platforms like AWS, Azure, and Google Cloud, microservices can be deployed in a way that they automatically scale up or down based on traffic or resource usage, providing greater efficiency in resource allocation.

2. Flexibility and Agility:

- **Faster Development Cycles:** Since microservices are small and focused on specific business capabilities, development teams can work autonomously on different services without stepping on each other's toes. This enables faster iterations and quicker releases of new features.

- **Independent Deployment:** Microservices can be deployed independently, meaning a new feature or bug fix can be released without having to redeploy the entire system. This accelerates the deployment process and reduces downtime.

3. Fault Isolation and Resilience:

- **Isolation of Failures:** One of the key benefits of microservices is fault isolation. If one microservice fails, it doesn't bring down the entire system. This is in contrast to monolithic applications, where a failure in one part can potentially affect the whole system.
- **Improved Reliability:** Microservices, with their independent deployment and isolation, allow for more robust and resilient systems. When a failure occurs in one service, it is easier to identify, fix, and restore the system to normal.

4. Technology Diversity and Innovation:

- **Choosing the Right Tool for the Job:** Microservices allow teams to choose the best technology for each service. For example, a service that requires high-speed processing might be built with C++, while another that handles complex data processing might be built using Python. This flexibility leads to innovation and allows developers to use the best tools for specific tasks.
- **Evolving Technologies:** As new technologies emerge, microservices offer an easy way to adopt them. Teams can swap out one microservice with a newer, more efficient version without impacting the rest of the application.

5. Organizational Benefits:

- **Autonomous Teams:** Microservices enable the formation of cross-functional teams responsible for specific services. This autonomy leads to better collaboration, faster decision-making, and a more efficient development process.
- **Alignment with Business Functions:** Each microservice is often aligned with a specific business capability or domain (e.g., order processing, payment handling). This helps ensure that development is closely aligned with business goals and priorities.

6. DevOps and Continuous Delivery:

- **Automation:** The use of microservices aligns well with DevOps practices, where automation plays a key role. Microservices enable automated testing, continuous integration, and continuous delivery (CI/CD) processes. Each microservice can be tested and deployed independently, speeding up the release cycle.
- **Improved CI/CD Pipelines:** With microservices, CI/CD pipelines can be optimized for individual services, reducing the overhead and ensuring faster delivery of features and fixes.

Summary:

In this chapter, we've traced the evolution of software architecture, from monolithic applications to Service-Oriented Architecture (SOA) and finally to microservices. While monolithic applications and SOA were foundational approaches to structuring software, microservices represent a significant leap forward, offering greater scalability, flexibility, fault isolation, and faster development cycles.

The transition to microservices is driven by the need for more resilient and scalable systems, the desire for faster development and deployment cycles, and the ability to innovate with new technologies. As we move forward in the book, we will explore how to design, develop, and deploy microservices using Java, taking full advantage of these architectural benefits.

CHAPTER 3

CORE CONCEPTS IN MICROSERVICES

Service Boundaries, Autonomy, and Loose Coupling

1. Service Boundaries: In a microservices architecture, a service is a self-contained, independent unit of functionality that can be developed, deployed, and scaled independently. The concept of **service boundaries** refers to defining clear and distinct roles for each microservice. These boundaries ensure that each service is responsible for a specific business capability or task, and its scope is well-defined.

For example:

- A **payment service** handles everything related to payment processing.
- A **shipping service** manages the delivery and logistics of products.
- A **user service** could be responsible for managing user accounts and authentication.

Why are service boundaries important?

- **Scalability**: Clear boundaries allow teams to scale individual services based on demand. For instance, if the payment service faces heavy traffic during peak times, it can be scaled independently of the other services.

- **Maintainability**: When services are independent and focused on a specific function, it becomes easier to modify or upgrade a service without impacting the rest of the system.

- **Autonomy**: Service boundaries ensure that each service can operate independently, meaning teams can work on different services concurrently without interfering with each other's work.

Real-World Example: Consider an online e-commerce platform. The **order service** could handle order creation and tracking, the **inventory service** would manage stock levels, and the **payment service** would process transactions. By establishing clear boundaries, each service can evolve independently, be deployed separately, and can be modified without disrupting the entire application.

2. Autonomy: Autonomy means that each microservice can function independently, both in terms of functionality and its own resources. It has its own data, business logic, and management responsibilities. Autonomy allows each service to be developed and deployed without depending on other services for its core functions.

31

Why is autonomy crucial?

- **Independence in development and deployment**: Each team can work on its service without worrying about other teams or services.
- **Faster time-to-market**: Changes in one service don't require testing or deploying the entire application.
- **Resilience**: If one service fails, the other services can continue to operate normally.

3. Loose Coupling: Loose coupling refers to minimizing dependencies between services. In a microservices architecture, services communicate with one another through well-defined APIs or messaging systems, but they don't directly depend on each other's internal implementation details. This isolation means that services can evolve independently without introducing bugs or breaking other parts of the system.

Benefits of loose coupling:

- **Flexibility**: Services can be modified, upgraded, or replaced without impacting other services.
- **Fault tolerance**: The failure of one service doesn't directly affect the operation of other services.
- **Simplified maintenance**: Since each service is independent, managing and debugging services is easier.

Real-World Example: In a microservices architecture for a ride-sharing platform, the **payment service** should be loosely coupled from the **ride-matching service**. If the payment service has a bug or is down, the ride-matching service should still be able to find rides for customers and drivers without interruption.

Communication Patterns: Synchronous vs. Asynchronous

1. Synchronous Communication: In **synchronous communication**, one service makes a request to another service and waits for a response before continuing. This is similar to a traditional function call: the calling service is blocked until it gets a response from the other service.

Characteristics of synchronous communication:

- **Request-response pattern:** The calling service sends a request, and the callee sends a response back. This communication typically happens via HTTP (RESTful APIs) or gRPC.
- **Blocking:** The caller waits for the response before continuing its execution.
- **Tightly coupled:** Services are tightly coupled in terms of the request-response cycle.

When to use synchronous communication:

- When a service needs immediate feedback to proceed with its workflow.
- For critical processes like real-time user requests, such as processing a payment or booking a ride.

Example:

- A **payment service** might use synchronous communication when a customer is making a payment. The payment service will need to immediately verify the transaction and return a result (success or failure) to the requesting system, such as the e-commerce checkout system.

2. Asynchronous Communication: Asynchronous communication allows services to send messages or requests without waiting for a direct response. Instead of blocking and waiting for a reply, the service sends the request and continues executing other tasks. The response is handled separately, often through a message queue or event-driven architecture.

Characteristics of asynchronous communication:

- **Message-based or event-driven**: Services send messages to a queue or publish events to an event bus. Other services can listen for these messages or events and act upon them when necessary.

- **Non-blocking**: The sending service does not wait for a response, allowing it to proceed with other tasks.
- **Loosely coupled**: Services are decoupled from each other since they do not depend on receiving a response.

When to use asynchronous communication:

- When responses are not immediately needed, and you want to avoid blocking the calling service.
- For tasks that can be processed later, such as sending emails, processing payments in the background, or updating analytics.

Example:

- In an e-commerce application, the **order service** might asynchronously send an event to a **shipping service** to begin the fulfillment process after an order is placed. The order service doesn't need to wait for a response and can continue processing other orders.

Key Tools for Asynchronous Communication:

- **Message Queues**: Tools like **RabbitMQ**, **Apache Kafka**, or **ActiveMQ** are commonly used to handle asynchronous communication by queuing messages for later processing.

- **Event-driven Architectures**: **Event sourcing** and **CQRS (Command Query Responsibility Segregation)** are patterns that support asynchronous communication, particularly in systems that need to process large volumes of events or commands.

Real-World Example:

- In a **ride-sharing service**, when a user requests a ride, the request could be sent asynchronously to the ride-matching service. The user's app continues to work while the backend processes the ride-matching request in the background, reducing latency and improving the user experience.

Database Per Service: The Decentralized Approach

In a microservices architecture, each service typically manages its own **database** or data store, following the principle of **database per service**. This is a key aspect of the **decentralized approach** in microservices.

1. Why Use a Database Per Service?

- **Autonomy**: Since each microservice is autonomous, it requires its own database to ensure it can function independently of other services. This prevents any shared database dependencies and avoids the risk of tightly coupling services around a single database.

- **Scalability**: Each service can choose the best database technology that suits its needs. For example, a **user service** might use a relational database like MySQL for structured data, while a **logging service** might use a NoSQL database like MongoDB for unstructured data.

- **Fault Isolation**: If one service's database experiences issues, it does not affect the databases of other services. This isolation ensures that failures are contained and don't ripple through the entire system.

2. Challenges with Database per Service:

- **Data Consistency**: Ensuring consistency across multiple services' databases can be challenging. Since each microservice has its own data, keeping data consistent across services requires careful handling of transactions.

    o **Eventual Consistency**: Microservices generally embrace **eventual consistency**, where services may temporarily have inconsistent data but will eventually synchronize. This is often handled via messaging or event-driven systems.

- **Distributed Transactions**: In traditional monolithic applications, a single transaction might span multiple components. In microservices, however, each service has its own database, so managing transactions across multiple services can be tricky. The **SAGA pattern** is one way to handle distributed transactions by breaking them down into smaller, compensating transactions that ensure data consistency across services.

3. Example of Database per Service: Consider a **payment service** that uses a relational database to store transaction details, while an **inventory service** uses a NoSQL database to store stock levels. Since both services manage their own databases, they can be scaled and managed independently. The **inventory service** will have its own database of stock, and the **payment service** will have its own database of transactions, each designed to optimize the respective service's performance.

Real-World Example: A well-known example of database-per-service in microservices architecture is **Amazon**. Each service, like order management, customer management, and inventory, uses its own database technology best suited to its requirements. The **order service** might use a relational database for ACID transactions, while the **search service** might rely on Elasticsearch for quick search and retrieval.

Summary:

In this chapter, we explored some of the core concepts of microservices architecture: **service boundaries, autonomy, loose coupling, synchronous vs. asynchronous communication**, and the **database per service** principle.

We discussed how well-defined service boundaries allow each service to function independently, the importance of autonomy for scaling and fault isolation, and how loose coupling leads to greater flexibility and resilience. Communication in microservices can either be synchronous or asynchronous, each with its specific use cases and tools. Finally, the **database per service** approach is essential for maintaining autonomy and scalability but requires careful attention to data consistency and handling distributed transactions.

As we continue in the book, we will delve deeper into how these core concepts can be practically implemented in Java-based microservices, using tools like Spring Boot, Kafka, and Docker.

CHAPTER 4

SETTING UP YOUR DEVELOPMENT ENVIRONMENT

In this chapter, we will walk through the essential tools and technologies required to build Java-based microservices, guide you on how to set up your Integrated Development Environment (IDE), and introduce version control best practices. These tools will help streamline your microservices development and enable an efficient and collaborative workflow.

Tools and Technologies Required for Building Java-Based Microservices

1. Java Development Kit (JDK):

- The **JDK** is the cornerstone of any Java-based development, as it contains the core libraries and compilers needed to build Java applications. To develop microservices in Java, you need a suitable version of the JDK.

- For microservices, **JDK 8** or later versions (JDK 11, JDK 17) are highly recommended due to their long-term support and advanced features. Java 17, for instance, offers better performance and enhanced features like

40

pattern matching, records, and the new `sealed` classes that can help in more efficient code structuring for microservices.

How to Install JDK:

- Download the JDK from **Oracle's official website** or use **OpenJDK**, an open-source version of the JDK.
- Install the JDK on your system by following the installation steps for your platform (Windows, macOS, or Linux).
- After installation, ensure that your system's **environment variables** (such as `JAVA_HOME`) are properly set to the JDK directory.

2. Maven:

- **Apache Maven** is a build automation tool used primarily for Java projects. It simplifies project management by providing dependency management, building, testing, and packaging functionality. With Maven, you can automate the building of your Java microservices and handle libraries and dependencies efficiently.

How to Install Maven:

- Download Maven from the official **Apache Maven website**.

41

- Follow the installation instructions to configure **MAVEN_HOME** and update the system PATH.
- Maven integrates seamlessly with **Spring Boot** and other tools to manage your microservices dependencies.

3. Spring Boot:

- **Spring Boot** is one of the most popular frameworks for building Java-based microservices. It simplifies the setup and configuration of microservices and is widely used because of its **ease of use** and **wide ecosystem**.
- With **Spring Boot**, you can create stand-alone, production-ready Spring-based applications with minimal configuration. It includes embedded servers like **Tomcat**, **Jetty**, and **Undertow**, so you don't need to deploy your microservices on external application servers.

Why Spring Boot?

- **Quick Setup**: You can quickly bootstrap a microservice project with minimal configurations.
- **Embedded Servers**: Spring Boot includes an embedded HTTP server (Tomcat by default), so there's no need to install a separate web server.
- **Microservices Support**: Spring Boot works seamlessly with other Spring projects like **Spring Cloud**, which

provides tools for building distributed systems and microservices.

How to Set Up Spring Boot:

- Use **Spring Initializr** (https://start.spring.io/) to quickly generate a Spring Boot project. You can select dependencies, such as Spring Web, Spring Data, and Spring Security, based on your project needs.
- Add dependencies to your `pom.xml` file (for Maven) or `build.gradle` (for Gradle) to integrate Spring Boot libraries and features.
- For a quick test, you can run your microservice directly from your IDE using the Spring Boot run configuration or the command line using `mvn spring-boot:run`.

4. Docker (Optional but Recommended for Containerization):

- **Docker** allows you to containerize your microservices, providing a consistent environment for development, testing, and production.
- Using Docker, you can package your microservices into isolated containers that run anywhere—whether on your local machine or in the cloud.

5. Testing Frameworks:

- **JUnit**: JUnit is the standard testing framework for Java and is used to create unit tests for your microservices.
- **Mockito**: Mockito is a popular mocking framework that helps you isolate units of code during testing, which is especially useful for testing individual microservices in isolation.
- **Spring Test**: For integration testing of Spring Boot-based microservices, you can use **Spring Test** to write tests that validate your services.

IDE Setup (IntelliJ IDEA, Eclipse)

1. IntelliJ IDEA:

- **IntelliJ IDEA** is a powerful, feature-rich IDE specifically designed for Java development. It is popular for building microservices because of its integrated support for Spring Boot and other related technologies.
- IntelliJ IDEA offers smart code completion, refactoring tools, version control integration, and more. It also integrates with tools like Docker, Maven, and Gradle, which are essential for microservices development.

How to Set Up IntelliJ IDEA:

- Download the community or ultimate edition of **IntelliJ IDEA** from the official website.

44

- Install the **Spring Boot** plugin for full support in developing Spring-based applications.
- Create a new **Spring Boot project** by selecting the appropriate project template and dependencies (such as Spring Web, Spring Data, and Spring Boot DevTools for live reloading).
- Use the **Maven** or **Gradle** build tool integration within IntelliJ IDEA to handle dependencies and build automation.

2. Eclipse:

- **Eclipse** is another popular IDE for Java development. It provides a robust set of features for Java, including support for **Maven** and **Gradle**, and integrates with **Spring Tools** (formerly known as Spring IDE) to simplify Spring Boot development.

How to Set Up Eclipse:

- Download and install **Eclipse IDE for Java Developers** from the official website.
- Install the **Spring Tools** plugin to get full support for Spring Boot development.
- Use **Maven** or **Gradle** to manage dependencies and set up your project.

- Eclipse's **Java EE** features can be used for building RESTful APIs and microservices.

Which IDE Should You Choose?

- If you're focused on building **Spring Boot-based** microservices, **IntelliJ IDEA** is often the preferred choice due to its built-in support for Spring and ease of use. However, **Eclipse** can still be a good choice, especially if you're familiar with it or prefer an open-source solution.

Version Control Systems (e.g., Git) and Best Practices

1. Git:

- **Git** is the most widely used version control system for managing source code. It allows teams to collaborate efficiently by tracking changes to the codebase and providing the ability to revert to previous versions if needed.
- Git is essential for managing microservices projects because it enables distributed development. With multiple teams working on different services, Git allows each team to independently commit, merge, and track changes to their respective services.

How to Set Up Git:

- Download **Git** from the official Git website and follow the installation instructions for your operating system.
- Configure your **Git identity** by setting your username and email via the command line:

arduino

```
git config --global user.name "Your Name"
git config --global user.email
"youremail@example.com"
```

- Use **GitHub**, **GitLab**, or **Bitbucket** to host your repositories and manage collaborations.
- Clone a repository with the command:

bash

```
git clone https://github.com/your-
repository-url.git
```

2. Git Workflow for Microservices:

- **Branching**: Use **feature branches** for each new microservice or feature development. This isolates new changes from the main branch until they are ready to be merged.
- **Pull Requests**: Once your feature or service is ready, create a **pull request (PR)** to merge your changes into the

47

main branch. This allows team members to review code before it is integrated.

- **Commit Messages**: Write clear and descriptive commit messages that explain why changes were made. Use conventional commit formats such as:

```makefile
makefile


feat: add payment service
fix: bug fix in inventory service
docs:   update   README   for   deployment
instructions
```

- **CI/CD Integration**: Git repositories can integrate with **Continuous Integration** and **Continuous Deployment** (CI/CD) systems like **Jenkins, CircleCI**, or **GitHub Actions**. These systems automatically run tests and deploy code changes, helping to maintain a smooth and error-free deployment pipeline.

3. Best Practices for Version Control:

- **Modularization**: Keep each microservice in a separate repository, or use **mono repos** with clear boundaries for each microservice. This helps avoid unnecessary interdependencies.

- **Versioning**: Use **semantic versioning** (e.g., v1.0.0) for your microservices to track changes over time and ensure compatibility between services.
- **Commit Early, Commit Often**: Small, frequent commits are preferable to large, infrequent ones. This reduces the risk of conflicts and helps maintain a clean and understandable history.

Real-World Example:

- In a microservices-based e-commerce application, you might have separate Git repositories for the **user service**, **order service**, **payment service**, and **inventory service**. Each service would be developed, tested, and deployed independently, while version control ensures that all teams can work in parallel without interfering with each other's code.

Summary:

In this chapter, we've explored the essential tools and technologies needed to set up your Java-based microservices development environment. We covered the **JDK**, **Maven**, **Spring Boot**, **Docker** (optional), and testing frameworks that will serve as the backbone of your microservices applications.

We also discussed setting up your **IDE** (either IntelliJ IDEA or Eclipse), choosing the right one based on your needs and preferences. Lastly, we covered **version control systems**, with a focus on **Git** and best practices for using Git in microservices development. This setup ensures efficient collaboration and smooth development cycles as you build, test, and deploy your microservices.

In the next chapters, we will dive deeper into creating and managing microservices, testing, securing, and deploying them effectively.

CHAPTER 5

BUILDING YOUR FIRST MICROSERVICE WITH JAVA AND SPRING BOOT

In this chapter, we will walk through building your first microservice using **Spring Boot**, a powerful and widely used framework for Java development. We will guide you step-by-step through creating a simple **RESTful service** and cover the application structure, key annotations, and configuration that will help you get up and running with microservices development.

Introduction to Spring Boot for Microservices Development

Spring Boot is a framework designed to simplify the setup and development of Java applications, particularly for microservices. It builds on the **Spring Framework** by providing a more streamlined approach to creating standalone, production-ready applications. With **Spring Boot**, you don't have to worry about complex configurations, as it auto-configures many aspects of your application based on the dependencies you add.

Why Use Spring Boot for Microservices?

- **Quick Setup:** Spring Boot provides a convention-over-configuration approach, which helps you get started quickly. You can create a microservice with minimal effort, reducing boilerplate code and configuration overhead.

- **Embedded Servers:** Spring Boot includes embedded web servers (like **Tomcat**), meaning you don't need to install or configure an external server. The application can run as a stand-alone executable JAR file.

- **Microservices-Oriented Features:** Spring Boot integrates seamlessly with **Spring Cloud**, a set of tools that help you develop distributed systems and microservices.

Spring Boot is widely adopted because it simplifies development, provides powerful tools for building scalable applications, and integrates well with other tools for monitoring, security, and deployment.

Step-by-Step Guide to Creating a Simple RESTful Service

In this section, we will walk through building a simple **RESTful web service** with Spring Boot. This service will expose a **GET endpoint** that returns a message when accessed.

Step 1: Create a Spring Boot Project

52

- The easiest way to generate a Spring Boot project is by using **Spring Initializr**, which is available at https://start.spring.io/. This online tool allows you to create a Maven or Gradle-based project with the required dependencies.

Here's how to generate the project:

- **Project:** Choose **Maven Project** (or Gradle if preferred).
- **Language:** Choose **Java**.
- **Spring Boot Version:** Use the default (the latest stable release).
- **Group:** Enter your preferred group name, e.g., `com.example`.
- **Artifact:** Enter the artifact name, e.g., `hello-world`.
- **Dependencies:** Select **Spring Web** (this provides support for building web applications).

Click **Generate**, and the project will be downloaded as a ZIP file. Extract the contents and open it in your IDE (IntelliJ IDEA or Eclipse).

Step 2: Define the Controller A **RESTful service** in Spring Boot is typically built using the `@RestController` annotation, which is part of Spring Web. The controller will handle HTTP requests and return appropriate responses.

Create a new Java class called `HelloController.java` in the `src/main/java/com/example/helloworld` directory (or the package structure you specified in the Spring Initializr).

```java

package com.example.helloworld;

import org.springframework.web.bind.annotation.GetMapping;
import org.springframework.web.bind.annotation.RestController;

@RestController
public class HelloController {

    @GetMapping("/hello")
    public String sayHello() {
        return "Hello, World!";
    }
}
```

Explanation:

- `@RestController`: Marks this class as a controller that handles HTTP requests and automatically serializes the return values to JSON (or plain text).

- `@GetMapping("/hello")`: Maps the `/hello` endpoint to the `sayHello()` method. This method will return a string message, "Hello, World!" when a **GET** request is made to this endpoint.

Step 3: Run the Application

- Inside your project directory, you will find a class named `HelloWorldApplication.java`. This is the main entry point of your Spring Boot application.

```java
package com.example.helloworld;

import org.springframework.boot.SpringApplication;
import org.springframework.boot.autoconfigure.SpringBootApplication;

@SpringBootApplication
public class HelloWorldApplication {

    public static void main(String[] args) {

SpringApplication.run(HelloWorldApplication.class, args);
    }
```

```
}
```

The @SpringBootApplication annotation is a combination of several annotations that enable auto-configuration, component scanning, and configuration properties. When you run this class, Spring Boot will automatically start an embedded Tomcat server, hosting your microservice.

You can run the application directly from your IDE or via the command line:

- **Command line:** Navigate to the project directory and run:

  ```arduino```

  ```
  mvn spring-boot:run
  ```

  This will start the application and make it accessible on http://localhost:8080.

Step 4: Test the Service

- Open a browser or use a tool like **Postman** or **curl** to send a **GET request** to http://localhost:8080/hello.

You should see the response:
  ```

```
Hello, World!
```

This simple service is now up and running, returning a basic string message. In the next sections, we'll go into more complex functionality, but this forms the foundation of how Spring Boot microservices are created.

Understanding Application Structure, Annotations, and Configuration

Spring Boot applications have a specific directory and file structure. Let's take a look at the basic structure of the generated project and the key components:

1. Directory Structure:

css

```
hello-world/
├── src/
│   ├── main/
│   │   ├── java/
│   │   │   └── com/example/helloworld/
│   │   │       ├── HelloController.java
│   │   │       └── HelloWorldApplication.java
│   │   ├── resources/
│   │   │   ├── application.properties
│   │   │   └── static/
```

```
|   |   └── templates/
├── target/
├── pom.xml (Maven configuration file)
└── README.md
```

Key Files and Directories:

- **src/main/java/**: Contains the Java code for your microservices. In this case, HelloController.java and HelloWorldApplication.java are inside the com.example.helloworld package.
- **src/main/resources/**: Contains the application.properties file, where you can define your application configuration.
- **target/**: This directory contains the compiled bytecode and packaged JAR file when you build the project.
- **pom.xml**: The Maven configuration file, where you define dependencies and project settings.

2. Important Annotations:

- @RestController: Marks a class as a RESTful controller that can handle HTTP requests.
- @GetMapping: Maps HTTP GET requests to the sayHello() method.

- `@SpringBootApplication`: A convenience annotation that enables Spring Boot's auto-configuration, component scanning, and bean creation.

3. Application Configuration: Spring Boot allows you to configure your application through the **application.properties** file. This file is located under `src/main/resources/` and can hold properties like database configuration, logging settings, or server settings.

Example of basic `application.properties` configuration:

properties

```
server.port=8080
spring.application.name=HelloWorldService
logging.level.org.springframework.web=DEBUG
```

- `server.port`: Changes the port the application runs on (default is 8080).
- `spring.application.name`: Sets the name of your application.
- `logging.level.org.springframework.web=DEB UG`: Sets the logging level to DEBUG for the Spring Web package to help troubleshoot issues.

Summary:

In this chapter, we've walked through building your first **Java-based microservice** using **Spring Boot**. We covered the essential steps to:

- Set up a Spring Boot project using **Spring Initializr**.
- Build a simple **RESTful web service** with a `GET` endpoint using `@RestController` and `@GetMapping`.
- Understand the basic **application structure**, important **annotations**, and how to configure the application via the `application.properties` file.

This foundation sets the stage for more complex microservices development. As we continue, you'll learn how to add more advanced features, integrate databases, secure your services, and manage them in a distributed environment.

CHAPTER 6

SERVICE COMMUNICATION IN MICROSERVICES

In this chapter, we'll explore how services communicate with each other in a **microservices architecture**. One of the most common ways services interact is through **RESTful APIs**. We'll cover the basics of HTTP methods and status codes, explain why **JSON** is the standard format for communication, and demonstrate how to create APIs using **Spring Web** and **RestController**.

RESTful APIs: Basics of HTTP, Methods, Status Codes

1. What is REST? REST, or **Representational State Transfer**, is an architectural style for designing networked applications. It uses HTTP as its communication protocol and defines a set of constraints for creating APIs that are lightweight, scalable, and stateless.

RESTful APIs rely on HTTP methods to define actions on resources, and these resources are typically represented by URLs. REST is simple, uses standard HTTP protocols, and is highly scalable, making it an ideal choice for microservices communication.

2. HTTP Methods (Verbs): In RESTful APIs, communication between services is performed using HTTP methods. These methods map to CRUD operations (Create, Read, Update, Delete) and define how data is manipulated.

- **GET**: Retrieves data from a service. It is used for **read-only** operations and should not alter the state of the server.
    - o Example: `GET /products` retrieves all products from the product catalog.
- **POST**: Sends data to the server to create a new resource. It is typically used for **creating new entities**.
    - o Example: `POST /orders` creates a new order with the data sent in the request body.
- **PUT**: Updates an existing resource with the provided data. It is used to replace the entire resource.
    - o Example: `PUT /products/123` updates the product with ID 123 with new data.
- **PATCH**: Partially updates an existing resource. Unlike PUT, PATCH allows for **partial updates** without replacing the entire resource.
    - o Example: `PATCH /products/123` updates only the fields that are modified, such as price.
- **DELETE**: Removes a resource from the server.
    - o Example: `DELETE /products/123` deletes the product with ID 123 from the catalog.

3. HTTP Status Codes: HTTP status codes are part of the response sent by the server to indicate the result of an HTTP request. They help clients understand the outcome of their requests.

Here are some common status codes:

- **200 OK**: The request was successful, and the server returned the requested data.
    - o   Example: A successful GET request returns the data for the requested resource.
- **201 Created**: The request was successful, and a new resource was created. This is typically used with the POST method.
    - o   Example: A new POST /orders request that successfully creates an order.
- **400 Bad Request**: The server cannot process the request because the client sent invalid data.
    - o   Example: Sending invalid data in a POST request.
- **401 Unauthorized**: The client is not authenticated to access the requested resource.
    - o   Example: Trying to access a protected API without valid credentials.
- **404 Not Found**: The requested resource could not be found on the server.
    - o   Example: A GET request for /products/12345 returns this status if product 12345 doesn't exist.

- **500 Internal Server Error**: The server encountered an unexpected condition that prevented it from fulfilling the request.

  o Example: A database failure or unhandled exception on the server.

JSON as the Communication Format

1. Why JSON? In modern web services, **JSON (JavaScript Object Notation)** is the most commonly used format for sending data between services. Its simplicity and human-readable structure make it ideal for API communication. JSON is easy to parse and generate, which makes it compatible with a wide range of programming languages and platforms.

JSON Example: Here is an example of a JSON response returned by a product service:

json

```
{
  "id": 1,
  "name": "Laptop",
  "description": "High-performance laptop",
  "price": 1200.00
}
```

2. JSON and Microservices Communication: In microservices architectures, services communicate via HTTP requests and responses, and these exchanges often include JSON-encoded payloads. Services send and receive JSON objects as part of their API requests (using the HTTP POST, PUT, PATCH, or GET methods).

For example, when a **customer service** sends a request to the **order service** to create an order, the payload might be a JSON object containing details like customer ID, product ID, and quantity.

3. JSON in Spring Boot: Spring Boot automatically uses **Jackson** (a popular JSON library for Java) to serialize Java objects into JSON and deserialize JSON back into Java objects. This allows Spring Boot to easily handle JSON as both request bodies and response bodies.

Using Spring Web and RestController to Create APIs

1. Spring Web Overview: Spring Web is a module of the Spring Framework that provides tools and features for building web applications, including RESTful APIs. **Spring Boot** simplifies the configuration of Spring Web and helps you quickly set up APIs.

2. The `@RestController` Annotation: In Spring Boot, the `@RestController` annotation is used to mark a class as a RESTful controller. It combines the functionality of `@Controller` (which is used for traditional web applications) and `@ResponseBody` (which converts the return value into a response body). This means that methods in a `@RestController` return data (often in JSON format) rather than views.

Example: Here's an example of how to use Spring Boot to create a simple RESTful API:

```java
package com.example.productservice;

import
org.springframework.web.bind.annotation.GetMapp
ing;
import
org.springframework.web.bind.annotation.PathVar
iable;
import
org.springframework.web.bind.annotation.RestCon
troller;

@RestController
public class ProductController {
```

```
// GET /products/1
@GetMapping("/products/{id}")
public                              Product
getProduct(@PathVariable("id") Long id) {
    // Simulate retrieving a product from the
database
    return new Product(id, "Laptop", "High-
performance laptop", 1200.00);
    }
}
```

Explanation:

- @RestController: Marks the ProductController class as a REST controller, so its methods will handle HTTP requests and return data as JSON.

- @GetMapping("/products/{id}"): Maps the HTTP GET request for /products/{id} to the getProduct method. The {id} is a path variable that will be extracted and passed to the method.

- @PathVariable("id"): This annotation binds the value from the URL to the method parameter.

- Product: A simple Java class representing a product (you will define this class separately).

Product Model Example:

```java
java

package com.example.productservice;

public class Product {
    private Long id;
    private String name;
    private String description;
    private Double price;

    // Constructor, getters, and setters omitted for brevity

    public Product(Long id, String name, String description, Double price) {
        this.id = id;
        this.name = name;
        this.description = description;
        this.price = price;
    }
}
```

3. Testing the API:

- Once the application is running, you can test the GET /products/{id} endpoint by navigating to http://localhost:8080/products/1.
- The response would look like this (in JSON format):

```json
json

{
  "id": 1,
  "name": "Laptop",
  "description": "High-performance laptop",
  "price": 1200.00
}
```

4. Handling JSON Requests (POST, PUT, PATCH): Spring Boot makes it easy to handle JSON data in requests. For example, to handle a **POST** request where clients send JSON data to create a new product, you can define the following endpoint:

```java
java

package com.example.productservice;

import
org.springframework.web.bind.annotation.PostMap
ping;
import
org.springframework.web.bind.annotation.Request
Body;
import
org.springframework.web.bind.annotation.RestCon
troller;

@RestController
```

```
public class ProductController {

    // POST /products
    @PostMapping("/products")
    public Product createProduct(@RequestBody
Product product) {
        // Simulate saving the product
        return product;
    }
}
```

Explanation:

- `@PostMapping("/products")`: This maps the HTTP POST request for `/products` to the `createProduct` method.

- `@RequestBody`: This annotation tells Spring to deserialize the incoming JSON data into a `Product` object.

With this setup, a client can send a JSON request body like this:

json

```
{
  "name": "Smartphone",
  "description": "Latest model with high-end features",
  "price": 800.00
```

}

The response would return the same product data, simulating a product being created:

json

```json
{
  "id": 0,
  "name": "Smartphone",
  "description": "Latest model with high-end features",
  "price": 800.00
}
```

Summary:

In this chapter, we've covered the essential aspects of **service communication in microservices** using **RESTful APIs**. You learned about HTTP methods (GET, POST, PUT, PATCH, DELETE), status codes, and how **JSON** is used as the standard format for communication between services.

We also introduced the **Spring Web** module and demonstrated how to create a simple RESTful service using **@RestController** in Spring Boot. With these concepts in place, you are now ready to build more complex APIs, handle JSON data in requests and responses, and integrate additional functionality into your microservices.

As we progress through the book, we will expand on these concepts, adding security, data persistence, and more advanced features to your Spring Boot microservices.

CHAPTER 7

SECURING MICROSERVICES WITH OAUTH2 AND JWT

In this chapter, we will explore how to secure **microservices** by implementing **OAuth2** and **JSON Web Tokens (JWT)**, two essential components for **authentication** and **authorization**. Security is a critical aspect of any distributed system, and with microservices, ensuring that only authorized users and services can access specific resources is paramount. OAuth2 and JWT provide a robust framework for securing communication between microservices and their clients.

Authentication and Authorization in Microservices

Before diving into OAuth2 and JWT, it's important to understand the concepts of **authentication** and **authorization**, as these are the foundations of securing any microservices architecture.

1. Authentication: Authentication is the process of verifying the identity of a user or a system. In the context of microservices, authentication typically involves validating the credentials provided by a user (such as username and password) to confirm their identity.

73

- **Example**: When a user logs in to an application, the system authenticates their username and password to ensure they are who they claim to be.

2. Authorization: Authorization refers to the process of determining what actions an authenticated user or service is allowed to perform. Once the user or service is authenticated, the system grants or denies access to resources based on their roles, permissions, or other criteria.

- **Example**: A user may be authenticated but only authorized to view specific parts of an application based on their role (e.g., an admin vs. a regular user).

In a microservices environment, **authentication** and **authorization** need to be handled securely across multiple services, often with complex access rules. This is where **OAuth2** and **JWT** come into play.

How to Implement OAuth2 and JSON Web Tokens (JWT)

OAuth2: OAuth2 is an open standard for authorization. It allows a user to grant a third-party application limited access to their resources without sharing their credentials. OAuth2 is commonly used to enable secure delegated access to APIs, especially in microservices architectures where multiple services need to authenticate and authorize each other.

74

- **OAuth2 Grant Types:** OAuth2 defines several types of authorization flows (also known as "grant types") that determine how the token is issued. The most common grant types are:

    1. **Authorization Code Grant**: This is the most common flow used for web applications. It involves redirecting the user to an authorization server where they authenticate and grant access. The authorization server then redirects back to the application with an authorization code, which the application exchanges for an access token.

    2. **Client Credentials Grant**: This flow is used for machine-to-machine communication where one service needs to access another service's resources without a user being involved. It is ideal for service-to-service communication in microservices architectures.

    3. **Password Grant**: This flow allows users to directly provide their credentials to the authorization server to obtain an access token. It is typically used in cases where the user trusts the client app (e.g., mobile applications).

    4. **Implicit Grant**: This flow is used for client-side applications (like single-page applications) where the access token is issued directly to the client without an authorization code exchange.

75

JWT (JSON Web Tokens): JWT is a compact and self-contained way to securely transmit information between parties. A JWT is often used as an access token in OAuth2 implementations. It is a JSON object that is encoded and signed, and sometimes encrypted, to ensure that the data cannot be tampered with.

- **JWT Structure**: A JWT consists of three parts:
    o **Header**: Contains metadata about the token, such as the signing algorithm (e.g., HMAC, RSA).
    o **Payload**: Contains the claims (the information or data) you want to transmit. This could include user information or roles.
    o **Signature**: This is used to verify that the token has not been altered. It's created by signing the header and payload with a secret key (HMAC) or a private key (RSA).

How OAuth2 and JWT Work Together:

- In OAuth2, when a user successfully authenticates, the authorization server issues a **JWT token** (access token). The user's client can then use this JWT to make secure API requests to microservices.
- Each microservice can **verify** the JWT token to ensure the request is authorized and the user has the necessary permissions to access the requested resources.

Real-World Example: Securing a Service with OAuth2 and JWT

Let's walk through a real-world example of how to implement **OAuth2** and **JWT** for securing a microservice. In this example, we will secure an API that provides **product data**, ensuring that only authenticated and authorized users can access it.

Step 1: Set Up the Authorization Server (OAuth2)

The first step is to configure an **authorization server** that handles user authentication and issues **JWT tokens**. You can use **Spring Security OAuth2** to configure an authorization server.

Here is an example configuration of an OAuth2 Authorization Server in Spring Boot:

```java
@Configuration
@EnableAuthorizationServer
public class AuthorizationServerConfig extends
AuthorizationServerConfigurerAdapter {

    @Autowired
    private               AuthenticationManager
authenticationManager;

    @Override
```

```java
    public                              void
configure(AuthorizationServerEndpointsConfigure
r endpoints) {

endpoints.authenticationManager(authenticationM
anager)
                .tokenStore(tokenStore())

.accessTokenConverter(jwtAccessTokenConverter()
);
    }

    @Override
    public                              void
configure(ClientDetailsServiceConfigurer
clients) throws Exception {
        clients.inMemory()
                .withClient("clientApp")
                .secret("{noop}clientSecret")

.authorizedGrantTypes("password",
"refresh_token")
                .scopes("read")

.accessTokenValiditySeconds(3600); // 1 hour
    }

    @Bean
    public TokenStore tokenStore() {
```

```
    return                              new
JwtTokenStore(jwtAccessTokenConverter());
    }


    @Bean
    public                  JwtAccessTokenConverter
jwtAccessTokenConverter() {
        JwtAccessTokenConverter  converter  =  new
JwtAccessTokenConverter();
        converter.setSigningKey("secretKey"); //
Set the signing key
        return converter;
    }
}
```

Explanation:

- The `AuthorizationServerConfig` class sets up an OAuth2 authorization server.
- The `jwtAccessTokenConverter()` method defines how JWT tokens are signed with a `secretKey` (in a real-world app, you would likely use a private key instead of a simple secret).
- The client (`clientApp`) is configured to use the **password grant type**. The client will authenticate by sending the user's credentials (username/password) and will receive a JWT token in response.

Step 2: Set Up the Resource Server (API) to Secure the Service

Next, configure your **microservice** to act as a **resource server**, validating the JWT token before granting access to protected resources.

Here's an example of securing a REST API using Spring Security and JWT:

```java
@Configuration
@EnableWebSecurity
public class ResourceServerConfig extends
WebSecurityConfigurerAdapter {

    @Override
    protected void configure(HttpSecurity http)
throws Exception {
        http
            .authorizeRequests()

.antMatchers("/products/**").authenticated() //
Protect the /products endpoint
            .anyRequest().permitAll()
            .and()
            .oauth2Login(); // Enable OAuth2
login
    }

    @Override
```

```
    protected                          void
configure(AuthenticationManagerBuilder    auth)
throws Exception {

auth.authenticationProvider(authenticationProvi
der());
    }

    @Bean
    public                   JwtAuthenticationProvider
authenticationProvider() {
        return new JwtAuthenticationProvider();
    }
}
```

Explanation:

- In the `ResourceServerConfig` class, the `/products/**` endpoint is secured, meaning only authenticated users with a valid JWT can access it.
- The `oauth2Login()` method enables OAuth2 login for your microservice.
- A custom `JwtAuthenticationProvider` validates the incoming JWT token for each request to the `/products` endpoint.

Step 3: Creating the `ProductController`

Now that the authorization server and resource server are set up, let's create a simple RESTful API that is secured with OAuth2 and JWT.

java

```java
@RestController
@RequestMapping("/products")
public class ProductController {

    @GetMapping("/{id}")
    public Product getProduct(@PathVariable Long id) {
        // Simulate fetching a product by its ID
        return new Product(id, "Laptop", "High-performance laptop", 1200.00);
    }
}
```

Explanation:

- The /products/{id} endpoint is protected by OAuth2 and can only be accessed by clients with a valid JWT token. The microservice will verify the token before returning the product data.

Step 4: Testing the Security

To test the security, follow these steps:

1. First, authenticate by sending a POST request to the authorization server (e.g., /oauth/token) with the client credentials and user credentials (username/password).
2. The server will respond with a **JWT token**.
3. Use this JWT token as a bearer token in the **Authorization header** of the subsequent request to the /products/{id} endpoint.

Example of sending the token:

```bash
bash
```

```bash
curl -X GET "http://localhost:8080/products/1" -H "Authorization: Bearer {your-jwt-token}"
```

If the JWT token is valid, the server will return the requested product data. If the token is missing, invalid, or expired, the server will respond with a 401 Unauthorized error.

Summary:

In this chapter, we've learned how to secure microservices using **OAuth2** and **JWT**. We discussed the importance of **authentication** and **authorization** in microservices, and how to use **OAuth2** for authorization and **JWT** as a secure token format for communication between services.

We walked through the steps of setting up an **OAuth2 Authorization Server** that issues JWT tokens, configuring a **Resource Server** to secure an API endpoint, and testing the security with JWT. By implementing OAuth2 and JWT, you ensure that your microservices are both secure and scalable, with centralized authentication and distributed authorization.

As you continue building your microservices, these security practices will help safeguard your services from unauthorized access, ensuring that only valid users and services can interact with your system.

CHAPTER 8

MANAGING MICROSERVICES WITH SPRING CLOUD

In this chapter, we will explore **Spring Cloud**, a powerful set of tools that helps manage and build cloud-native applications, especially when dealing with microservices architectures. Spring Cloud simplifies the development of microservices-based applications by providing solutions for **service discovery**, **configuration management**, **routing**, and more. We will cover key components of the Spring Cloud ecosystem and show you how to set up these components to handle **service discovery** and **routing**.

Introduction to Spring Cloud and its Ecosystem

Spring Cloud is a set of tools and frameworks built on top of the **Spring Framework** that helps developers build distributed systems and microservices. It provides a comprehensive set of solutions for some of the most common challenges faced when building and deploying microservices in the cloud.

Key Benefits of Spring Cloud for Microservices:

1. **Service Discovery:** Automatically locate services in a distributed system, making it easy for microservices to communicate with each other.

2. **Routing and Load Balancing:** Dynamically route requests to available instances of a service and distribute traffic evenly across them.

3. **Centralized Configuration Management:** Manage configurations for all microservices from a central place, enabling flexible and consistent configurations across environments.

4. **Fault Tolerance:** Implement tools like circuit breakers to increase resilience in the system.

5. **Cloud-Native Development:** Spring Cloud supports the development of cloud-native applications, with built-in integrations for platforms like **Netflix OSS** and **Eureka**, **Consul**, and **Kubernetes**.

Spring Cloud works seamlessly with Spring Boot, and its components allow microservices to be built, deployed, and managed with minimal friction. It is designed to solve the common challenges in managing microservices at scale, such as service discovery, configuration management, and API routing.

Key Components of Spring Cloud

Spring Cloud provides several key components to address specific needs in microservices architectures. We will dive deeper into the following components:

1. Spring Cloud Config:

- **Spring Cloud Config** is used for **centralized configuration management**. It allows you to store the configurations of your microservices in a central repository (e.g., Git, SVN, or filesystem) and share them across all instances of your microservices.
- This is particularly useful when you have a large number of microservices with configurations that need to be consistent across all instances.

How Spring Cloud Config Works:

- The **Config Server** serves as a centralized source of configurations.
- Microservices can connect to the Config Server to retrieve their configuration at startup or dynamically during runtime.

Example Configuration:

- Store configuration files (like `application.yml` or `application.properties`) in a Git repository.
- The Config Server fetches these files and provides them to microservices.

```yaml
# application.yml in Git repository
spring:
  datasource:
    url: jdbc:mysql://localhost:3306/mydb
  server:
    port: 8080
```

- Microservices can retrieve these settings and update them dynamically without redeploying the service.

2. Eureka (Service Discovery):

- **Eureka** is a **service discovery** tool from the **Netflix OSS** suite, and it plays a crucial role in Spring Cloud.
- In a microservices architecture, services must be able to discover each other dynamically to enable communication between them. Eureka provides this capability by allowing services to register themselves and query the registry for other available services.

How Eureka Works:

- **Eureka Server**: Acts as the service registry where all microservices register themselves.
- **Eureka Client**: Microservices that need to find and interact with other services can query Eureka to get the available instances of those services.

Setting Up Eureka:

1. **Eureka Server**: A Spring Boot application acts as the Eureka server where microservices register themselves.
2. **Eureka Client**: Microservices can connect to the Eureka server to discover services using the `@EnableEurekaClient` annotation.

Eureka Server Example:

```java
@SpringBootApplication
@EnableEurekaServer
public class EurekaServerApplication {
    public static void main(String[] args) {

SpringApplication.run(EurekaServerApplication.class, args);
    }
}
```

Eureka Client Example:

```java

@SpringBootApplication
@EnableEurekaClient
public class ProductServiceApplication {
    public static void main(String[] args) {

SpringApplication.run(ProductServiceApplication
.class, args);
    }
}
```

3. Ribbon (Client-Side Load Balancer):

- **Ribbon** is a **client-side load balancer** that works with Eureka to distribute requests across multiple instances of a service. Ribbon automatically chooses the best available instance of a service based on configurable rules, such as round-robin or weighted load balancing.

How Ribbon Works:

- Ribbon can be integrated with **Eureka** to obtain a list of available service instances and distribute the traffic among them. Ribbon allows you to define how to balance traffic across instances, increasing the scalability and fault tolerance of your system.

Example Configuration with Ribbon:

```
yaml

spring:
  cloud:
    discovery:
      enabled: true
    loadbalancer:
      ribbon:
        enabled: true
```

In the **ProductService** example, when the product service needs to call another service (e.g., order service), Ribbon ensures that the traffic is distributed across available instances.

4. Zuul (API Gateway and Routing):

- **Zuul** is a **gateway** and **routing** tool that provides dynamic routing, monitoring, and security features for your microservices.
- Zuul acts as a reverse proxy that forwards client requests to appropriate microservices. It handles routing, load balancing, and security concerns, providing a central point for managing API traffic.

How Zuul Works:

- **Routing**: Zuul routes incoming HTTP requests to the appropriate microservices based on the URL path.

- **Load Balancing**: Zuul can integrate with Ribbon to load-balance requests across service instances.
- **Filters**: Zuul provides support for pre-filters, routing filters, and post-filters, enabling you to handle security, monitoring, and other concerns in a centralized manner.

Setting Up Zuul:

1. Add **Zuul** as a dependency in your `pom.xml` or `build.gradle`.
2. Enable Zuul routing in the Spring Boot application with the `@EnableZuulProxy` annotation.

Example Zuul Setup:

```java
@SpringBootApplication
@EnableZuulProxy
public class ApiGatewayApplication {
    public static void main(String[] args) {

SpringApplication.run(ApiGatewayApplication.class, args);
    }
}
```

Zuul Routing Configuration Example:

```yaml
yaml

zuul:
  routes:
    product-service: /products/**
    order-service: /orders/**
```

In this example, Zuul forwards requests starting with /products/** to the **product-service** and /orders/** to the **order-service**.

Setting Up Spring Cloud for Service Discovery and Routing

Now that we have an understanding of the key components, let's look at how to integrate **Eureka**, **Ribbon**, and **Zuul** into a microservices application for **service discovery** and **routing**.

1. Set Up Eureka for Service Discovery:

- Set up an **Eureka Server** to act as the service registry.
- Configure each microservice to register itself with Eureka using @EnableEurekaClient.

2. Set Up Zuul for API Gateway:

- Set up a Spring Boot application with **Zuul** to act as the API gateway.

- Use Zuul's routing capabilities to forward incoming requests to the appropriate services based on URL paths.
- Use Zuul in combination with **Ribbon** for client-side load balancing to ensure traffic is evenly distributed.

3. Enable Service Discovery in Other Microservices:

- Each microservice should be a **Eureka Client**, meaning they register themselves with the Eureka server and discover other services via Eureka.
- Microservices communicate using service names rather than hard-coded URLs. For example, to call the product service, instead of using a static URL like `http://localhost:8080/products`, you can use `http://product-service/products`, and **Ribbon** and **Eureka** will automatically discover and route the request to the appropriate service instance.

Summary:

In this chapter, we explored **Spring Cloud**, a suite of tools for managing microservices. We discussed the key components that make Spring Cloud powerful for managing distributed systems:

- **Spring Cloud Config** for centralized configuration management.

- **Eureka** for service discovery, allowing microservices to find and communicate with each other dynamically.
- **Ribbon** for client-side load balancing, ensuring requests are distributed across available service instances.
- **Zuul** for acting as an API Gateway, routing incoming client requests to the appropriate services and managing concerns like load balancing and security.

By combining these components, we can easily set up **service discovery** and **routing** in a microservices architecture. These tools make it much easier to manage microservices at scale, ensuring that services can dynamically discover each other, route requests efficiently, and remain resilient to failures.

In the following chapters, we will continue to explore how to deploy, scale, and secure these microservices, ensuring they are production-ready.

CHAPTER 9

DATABASE INTEGRATION IN MICROSERVICES

In this chapter, we will explore how **databases** are integrated within a **microservices architecture**. Unlike traditional monolithic applications, where a single database is typically shared by all components, **microservices** embrace a decentralized approach where each service manages its own database. This chapter will cover the concepts behind **database per service**, how microservices interact with their own databases, and how they communicate with each other in a distributed environment. Additionally, we will walk through a **real-world example** of integrating a database into a microservice.

How Each Microservice Manages Its Own Database

In a **monolithic architecture**, the application usually has a single, centralized database that all components of the application interact with. However, in a **microservices architecture**, each service is responsible for managing its own **database**, meaning each service will have its own **data store** that it controls.

This principle is known as **Database per Service**, and it's one of the core tenets of microservices architectures. There are several key reasons for this approach:

1. Autonomy and Independence:

- Each microservice is **independent** and **autonomous**. By having its own database, a service is fully in control of how it stores and accesses its data without relying on other services.
- Changes made to the database schema of one service do not affect other services, allowing teams to evolve and deploy services independently.

2. Flexibility in Data Storage:

- Microservices can choose the **best data storage solution** for their specific needs. For example, one microservice may use a **relational database** (e.g., MySQL or PostgreSQL) for structured data, while another may use a **NoSQL database** (e.g., MongoDB or Cassandra) for unstructured data.
- This flexibility allows teams to optimize their databases for the specific requirements of the service.

3. Scalability and Fault Isolation:

- By decentralizing the data storage, each service can scale independently. If one service experiences a high volume of requests, it can scale its database without affecting other services.

- Additionally, failures in one database do not impact the entire system, which enhances **resilience** and ensures that the failure of one microservice doesn't bring down the whole application.

Challenges of Database per Service:

- **Data Consistency:** Managing data consistency across services can be difficult. Since each microservice has its own database, maintaining consistent data across services becomes a complex task.

- **Distributed Transactions:** In a microservices architecture, performing a transaction across multiple services' databases (e.g., an order and payment service) requires careful handling.

Communication Between Microservices and Databases

Microservices need to interact with their respective databases and with each other to exchange data. There are two key types of communication that take place:

1. Service to Database Communication: Each microservice communicates with its own database through its local database client, typically via **JDBC** (for relational databases) or **NoSQL drivers** (for non-relational databases). The communication between a service and its database is relatively straightforward since each service owns its database.

Example: In a **Product Service**, you would use Spring Data JPA or JDBC templates to interact with a relational database (like MySQL):

```java
@Repository
public interface ProductRepository extends
JpaRepository<Product, Long> {
    List<Product>          findByCategory(String
category);
}
```

This approach allows the **Product Service** to manage its product data independently without affecting any other service's database.

2. Service to Service Communication: Microservices often need to communicate with each other to share data. The communication can be **synchronous** (using REST APIs) or **asynchronous** (using messaging queues like RabbitMQ or Kafka). These interactions allow one microservice to send requests to another and retrieve data, often through HTTP-based APIs.

However, in a **Database per Service** architecture, each service should avoid directly accessing another service's database. Instead, services exchange data via **APIs** or **events**, adhering to the **API Contract** established between the services.

For example, if an **Order Service** needs to know about the product details from the **Product Service**, it would make a REST API call rather than directly querying the product database.

Real-World Example: Integrating a Database with a Microservice

Let's go through a **real-world example** of integrating a database into a microservice. Suppose we have an **Order Service** that needs to store order information in a relational database (like PostgreSQL).

Step 1: Define the Database Model First, we define the **Order entity** in our service. In a Spring Boot application, we can use **Spring Data JPA** to define an entity that represents the order.

```java
@Entity
public class Order {
```

```
@Id
@GeneratedValue(strategy                    =
GenerationType.IDENTITY)
    private Long id;

    private String customerName;
    private String product;
    private Integer quantity;
    private Double price;

    // Getters and setters
}
```

Step 2: Create the Repository Next, we create a **repository** interface to interact with the database. Spring Data JPA automatically provides the implementation for CRUD operations.

```
java

@Repository
public    interface    OrderRepository    extends
JpaRepository<Order, Long> {
    List<Order>            findByCustomerName(String
customerName);
}
```

Step 3: Implement the Service Logic In the **Order Service**, we'll write the service logic to handle business logic related to orders.

java

```java
@Service
public class OrderService {

    @Autowired
    private OrderRepository orderRepository;

    public Order createOrder(Order order) {
        return orderRepository.save(order);
    }

    public                            List<Order>
getOrdersByCustomer(String customerName) {
        return
orderRepository.findByCustomerName(customerName
);
    }
}
```

Step 4: Expose the Order API We will expose a **RESTful API** in the **Order Service** to create and fetch orders.

java

```
@RestController
@RequestMapping("/orders")
public class OrderController {

    @Autowired
    private OrderService orderService;

    @PostMapping
    public                    ResponseEntity<Order>
createOrder(@RequestBody Order order) {
        Order          createdOrder          =
orderService.createOrder(order);
        return                          new
ResponseEntity<>(createdOrder,
HttpStatus.CREATED);
    }

    @GetMapping("/customer/{customerName}")
    public                         List<Order>
getOrdersByCustomer(@PathVariable       String
customerName) {
        return
orderService.getOrdersByCustomer(customerName);
    }
}
```

Step 5: Configure the Database In the
`application.properties` or `application.yml` file, we
configure the connection to the **PostgreSQL** database:

```
properties
```

```
spring.datasource.url=jdbc:postgresql://localho
st:5432/orders_db
spring.datasource.username=postgres
spring.datasource.password=yourpassword
spring.jpa.hibernate.ddl-auto=update
spring.jpa.show-sql=true
spring.jpa.properties.hibernate.dialect=org.hib
ernate.dialect.PostgreSQLDialect
```

This configuration ensures that Spring Boot will automatically set up a connection to the **PostgreSQL** database and manage the database schema.

Step 6: Testing the API Once the application is running, you can test the **Order Service** using **Postman** or **curl** to perform CRUD operations.

- To create a new order:

```bash
bash
```

```
curl -X POST "http://localhost:8080/orders" -H
"Content-Type:        application/json"        -d
'{"customerName":    "John    Doe",    "product":
"Laptop", "quantity": 2, "price": 1200.00}'
```

- To get orders by customer:

104

```bash
bash
```

```
curl "http://localhost:8080/orders/customer/John
Doe"
```

These requests will interact with the PostgreSQL database, creating and retrieving **Order** entities.

Key Considerations for Database Integration in Microservices

1. **Database per Service:** As mentioned earlier, each service should manage its own database. This ensures that each service is fully autonomous and does not share data with others via direct database queries.

2. **Data Consistency:** Since microservices have separate databases, it can be challenging to ensure data consistency. Techniques such as **eventual consistency**, **saga patterns**, or **two-phase commit** can be used to maintain data integrity across services.

3. **Data Duplication:** In some cases, services may need to duplicate data in their own databases. For example, the **Order Service** may store a **product ID**, but it doesn't need to store the entire product details. The **Product Service** will store the full product details. This duplication helps with service autonomy and scalability.

105

4. **API Integration:** Instead of direct database communication, microservices should interact with each other via **APIs** or **events**. This ensures that each service remains decoupled and allows for easier maintenance and scalability.

Summary

In this chapter, we explored how databases are integrated into microservices and how the **Database per Service** pattern ensures that each microservice manages its own data. We learned how to configure a **PostgreSQL** database with **Spring Data JPA**, implement a simple **Order Service**, and expose a **RESTful API** to create and retrieve orders.

We also discussed the challenges of managing data in a microservices architecture, including **data consistency** and **eventual consistency**. By following the **Database per Service** pattern and using APIs for communication between services, microservices remain independent and scalable, with each service controlling its own data and state.

In the following chapters, we will dive deeper into more advanced topics, including how to ensure **data consistency** across microservices, and how to implement **asynchronous communication** for more complex workflows.

CHAPTER 10

ASYNCHRONOUS MESSAGING WITH KAFKA

In this chapter, we will delve into the concept of **asynchronous messaging** and explore how **Kafka** serves as a robust **message broker** for enabling asynchronous communication between microservices. We will understand the fundamentals of **event-driven architecture**, the benefits of asynchronous communication, and how to implement Kafka to facilitate smooth communication in a microservices environment.

Introduction to Message Brokers and Kafka

Message Brokers: A **message broker** is an intermediary system that facilitates the communication between different services or applications by transmitting messages. In a **microservices architecture**, services often need to exchange information in a decoupled, asynchronous manner. A message broker allows these services to send, receive, and manage messages without directly invoking each other's APIs, thereby promoting loose coupling and increased system resilience.

The key role of a message broker in microservices is to decouple the services, allowing them to operate independently while ensuring that data is communicated effectively between them. Some common message brokers include:

- **RabbitMQ**
- **ActiveMQ**
- **Amazon SQS**
- **Apache Kafka**

Apache Kafka: Apache Kafka is a distributed event streaming platform, primarily designed for high-throughput, low-latency messaging. Kafka was initially developed by **LinkedIn** and later open-sourced. It is widely used for building real-time data pipelines and streaming applications.

Kafka is highly scalable and fault-tolerant, and it allows microservices to publish events (messages) to topics, which are then consumed by other services. Kafka's ability to handle large volumes of messages in real-time makes it ideal for applications requiring fast, reliable, and persistent message passing between microservices.

Key Concepts in Kafka:

- **Producer:** A producer is a component that sends messages (events) to a Kafka topic.

- **Consumer:** A consumer is a component that reads messages (events) from a Kafka topic.

- **Topic:** A Kafka topic is a category or channel to which producers send messages and from which consumers receive messages.

- **Partition:** A topic can be split into multiple partitions for parallel processing and horizontal scaling.

- **Consumer Group:** A group of consumers that share the load of reading from a topic. Each consumer in a group reads a unique subset of messages.

- **Broker:** Kafka brokers manage the storage and transmission of messages in a Kafka cluster.

Event-Driven Architecture: Benefits of Async Communication

Event-Driven Architecture (EDA): An **event-driven architecture (EDA)** is a design pattern in which the system reacts to events. In an EDA, **events** represent significant state changes, actions, or triggers that happen within the system, such as a user placing an order, a payment being processed, or a product being updated.

In an event-driven system, microservices publish events that other services can consume to react to or process those events. This design pattern is naturally suited for distributed systems like

110

microservices, where services are independent and should be loosely coupled.

Key Benefits of Asynchronous Communication:

1. **Decoupling:** Services do not need to be aware of each other's state or existence. This decoupling reduces dependencies and improves system flexibility and maintainability.

2. **Scalability:** With asynchronous communication, services can handle a large number of requests without blocking or waiting for responses from other services. This improves the system's ability to scale horizontally.

3. **Fault Tolerance:** If one service is unavailable, events can be stored in the message broker (like Kafka) and processed later. This helps ensure that no events are lost and that the system remains resilient.

4. **Performance Improvement:** Asynchronous communication allows services to perform other tasks while waiting for an event to be processed, reducing idle time and improving overall system performance.

5. **Real-Time Processing:** Kafka is designed to handle large volumes of messages in real-time, making it ideal for scenarios where near-instantaneous processing of events is critical.

Real-World Example of Asynchronous Communication:

- Consider an e-commerce platform where a user places an order. The order service can asynchronously send an event (such as `OrderPlaced`) to a Kafka topic. Other services, such as **inventory service**, **payment service**, and **shipping service**, consume this event and process it asynchronously. This allows each service to operate independently while reacting to the same event, ensuring that the entire order processing flow is handled efficiently.

Implementing Kafka for Microservices Communication

Now that we've covered the concepts of message brokers and event-driven architecture, let's look at how to implement **Kafka** for asynchronous communication in a microservices environment.

1. Setting Up Kafka: To use Kafka in your Spring Boot application, you need to set up a **Kafka broker**. Kafka brokers are responsible for storing and managing Kafka topics. You can either use a managed Kafka service, like **Amazon MSK** or **Confluent Cloud**, or set up your own Kafka cluster.

Here's how to install and run **Kafka locally**:

- Install **Apache Kafka** by following the instructions on the Kafka website.

- Once Kafka is installed, start **Zookeeper** (which Kafka depends on for managing cluster metadata) and then start the Kafka broker.

bash

```
# Start Zookeeper
bin/zookeeper-server-start.sh
config/zookeeper.properties

# Start Kafka
bin/kafka-server-start.sh
config/server.properties
```

2. Add Kafka Dependencies to Spring Boot: To integrate Kafka with your Spring Boot application, add the following dependencies to your **pom.xml** (for Maven) or **build.gradle** (for Gradle):

xml

```
<dependency>

<groupId>org.springframework.kafka</groupId>
    <artifactId>spring-kafka</artifactId>
</dependency>
```

3. Configuring Kafka in Spring Boot: Once Kafka is set up and the dependencies are added, you need to configure Kafka in your Spring Boot application.

In the **application.properties** or **application.yml**, add the Kafka configuration:

```properties

spring.kafka.bootstrap-servers=localhost:9092
spring.kafka.consumer.group-id=order-service
spring.kafka.consumer.auto-offset-reset=earliest
```

- `spring.kafka.bootstrap-servers`: Specifies the address of the Kafka broker.
- `spring.kafka.consumer.group-id`: Defines the consumer group for the Kafka consumers.
- `spring.kafka.consumer.auto-offset-reset`: Configures Kafka to start reading from the earliest message.

4. Kafka Producer: Sending Messages to a Topic In microservices, the **producer** is responsible for sending messages (events) to a Kafka topic. Let's implement a simple producer in Spring Boot that sends an event when an order is placed.

```java

```

```
import
org.springframework.kafka.core.KafkaTemplate;
import
org.springframework.kafka.annotation.EnableKafk
a;
import
org.springframework.beans.factory.annotation.Au
towired;
import
org.springframework.web.bind.annotation.PostMap
ping;
import
org.springframework.web.bind.annotation.Request
Body;
import
org.springframework.web.bind.annotation.RestCon
troller;

@RestController
@EnableKafka
public class OrderController {

    @Autowired
    private    KafkaTemplate<String,    String>
kafkaTemplate;

    private static final String TOPIC = "order-
placed";
```

```java
@PostMapping("/orders")
public void placeOrder(@RequestBody String
order) {
    // Send an event to the Kafka topic
    kafkaTemplate.send(TOPIC, order);
}
}
```

Explanation:

- `KafkaTemplate`: This is the primary class used for sending messages to Kafka topics.
- The `placeOrder` method sends an order message to the `order-placed` topic when a new order is placed.

5. Kafka Consumer: Consuming Messages from a Topic Now, we will set up a **Kafka consumer** that listens for events from the `order-placed` topic and processes them.

java

```java
import
org.springframework.kafka.annotation.KafkaListe
ner;
import org.springframework.stereotype.Service;

@Service
public class OrderEventListener {
```

```
@KafkaListener(topics = "order-placed",
groupId = "order-service")
    public void listenOrderEvent(String
orderEvent) {
        System.out.println("Received order
event: " + orderEvent);
        // Process the order event (e.g., update
inventory, initiate payment)
    }
}
```

Explanation:

- @KafkaListener: This annotation tells Spring to listen to the specified Kafka topic (order-placed) and invoke the method whenever a new message arrives.
- The listenOrderEvent method processes the event (e.g., updating inventory, initiating payment, etc.).

6. Testing the Kafka Setup: Once everything is set up, you can test the asynchronous communication:

1. Use a tool like **Postman** or **curl** to send a POST request to the /orders endpoint, which triggers the **OrderService** producer to send an event to Kafka.
2. The **OrderEventListener** consumer will automatically consume the message and process the order event.

117

Summary

In this chapter, we explored how **Kafka** enables **asynchronous messaging** in microservices architectures. We learned the benefits of **event-driven architecture**, including decoupling, scalability, fault tolerance, and real-time processing. Kafka plays a crucial role in implementing event-driven communication by providing a highly scalable and reliable way to pass messages between services.

We then implemented **Kafka** in a Spring Boot microservices application, setting up a **producer** to send messages to Kafka topics and a **consumer** to process those messages asynchronously. By adopting Kafka for communication, we can build more resilient, scalable, and loosely coupled microservices systems.

As we continue building microservices, Kafka's event-driven capabilities can be leveraged for a wide range of tasks, from processing user actions in real-time to integrating microservices in a distributed system.

CHAPTER 11

SERVICE DISCOVERY AND LOAD BALANCING

In this chapter, we will explore **service discovery** and **load balancing**, two essential patterns in a microservices architecture. Service discovery enables microservices to dynamically find each other, while load balancing ensures that requests are distributed efficiently across available service instances. We will focus on **Eureka** for service discovery, **Ribbon** for client-side load balancing, and **Zuul** for server-side load balancing.

Introduction to Service Discovery Patterns (Eureka)

In a **microservices** architecture, services are often distributed across multiple servers or containers. Since the number of instances and the locations of these services can change dynamically (e.g., services may scale up or down based on load), it's crucial for microservices to **discover** each other at runtime. This is where **service discovery** comes in.

Service Discovery allows microservices to dynamically register themselves when they start and deregister when they stop, ensuring that other services can find and communicate with them.

Eureka is one of the most popular tools for service discovery in the Spring ecosystem. It was developed by **Netflix** and is part of the **Netflix OSS** suite. Eureka provides a **service registry**, where microservices can register their information (like hostname, port, and health status). Other services can then query this registry to discover the available services.

How Eureka Works:

- **Eureka Server**: Acts as the service registry. Microservices register themselves with Eureka when they start up.
- **Eureka Client**: Microservices that need to discover other services query the Eureka server to retrieve the list of available instances of a service.

Key Features of Eureka:

- **Automatic Registration and Deregistration**: Services register with Eureka when they start and deregister when they shut down.
- **Heartbeat Mechanism**: Services send periodic heartbeats to Eureka to let it know that they are still alive. If Eureka doesn't receive a heartbeat for a while, it considers the service as **down**.

- **Client-Side Discovery**: Eureka enables clients to dynamically discover service instances and interact with them directly.

Setting Up Eureka:

1. **Eureka Server Configuration**:
   - In your Spring Boot application, add the `spring-cloud-starter-netflix-eureka-server` dependency to your `pom.xml` (for Maven).
   - Add `@EnableEurekaServer` annotation in the main class to configure it as a Eureka server.

```java
@SpringBootApplication
@EnableEurekaServer
public class EurekaServerApplication {
    public static void main(String[] args) {

SpringApplication.run(EurekaServerApplication.class, args);
    }
}
```

2. **Eureka Client Configuration**:

- o In your microservices, add the `spring-cloud-starter-netflix-eureka-client` dependency.
- o Enable Eureka client using `@EnableEurekaClient`.

java

```
@SpringBootApplication
@EnableEurekaClient
public class ProductServiceApplication {
    public static void main(String[] args) {

SpringApplication.run(ProductServiceApplication
.class, args);
    }
}
```

3. **Eureka Client Application Configuration** (`application.properties` or `application.yml`):

properties

```
eureka.client.serviceUrl.defaultZone=http
://localhost:8761/eureka/
spring.application.name=product-service
```

This configuration tells the microservice to register itself with the Eureka server at `http://localhost:8761/eureka/`.

Real-World Example: In a **shopping platform**, the **product service** registers itself with Eureka so that the **order service** can discover it and fetch product details. Similarly, **inventory services** and **payment services** register themselves for other services to discover them.

Client-Side Load Balancing with Ribbon

Load balancing is crucial in a microservices architecture, especially when a service has multiple instances running to handle high traffic. The goal of load balancing is to distribute incoming traffic efficiently across the available instances of a service.

Ribbon is a **client-side load balancer** that works in conjunction with **Eureka** to distribute requests among multiple instances of a service. It integrates with Spring Cloud and provides a **load balancing mechanism** directly on the client side.

How Ribbon Works:

- **Eureka** provides a list of available service instances.

- **Ribbon** dynamically chooses which instance to send the request to, using various load balancing strategies (e.g., round-robin, weighted response time, etc.).

Configuring Ribbon with Eureka:

1. **Add Ribbon Dependency**:
   - Ribbon is included in the `spring-cloud-starter-netflix-ribbon` dependency. If you're already using Eureka, Ribbon will be enabled automatically.

2. **Configuring Ribbon in the Client Application**:
   - Ribbon uses **service discovery** to fetch the list of available service instances from Eureka. It can load balance between those instances by default.

3. **Example of Using Ribbon for Load Balancing:** Let's say we have an **order service** that needs to call the **product service**. Instead of hardcoding the URL of the product service, we can use Ribbon to automatically load balance between instances of the product service.

```java
java


@RestController
public class OrderController {

    @Autowired
    private RestTemplate restTemplate;
```

124

```java
@RequestMapping("/order/{id}")
public                           String
getOrder(@PathVariable("id") Long orderId)
{
        // Ribbon    automatically    load
balances between available product service
instances
        return
restTemplate.getForObject("http://PRODUCT
-SERVICE/products/"        +        orderId,
String.class);
    }
}
```

@LoadBalanced RestTemplate: Ribbon works with **RestTemplate** in Spring Boot, and you need to annotate the **RestTemplate** bean with @LoadBalanced to enable client-side load balancing.

java

```java
@Configuration
public class RibbonConfig {

    @Bean
    @LoadBalanced
    public RestTemplate restTemplate() {
        return new RestTemplate();
```

```
        }

    }
```

Load Balancing Strategies: Ribbon offers different strategies for load balancing:

- **Round Robin**: The default strategy, which distributes requests evenly across all instances.
- **Weighted Response Time**: Instances with lower response times are given higher priority.
- **Random**: Distributes requests randomly.

Server-Side Load Balancing with Zuul

Zuul is a **server-side load balancer** and **API gateway** that provides routing and filtering capabilities in a microservices architecture. Unlike Ribbon, which performs load balancing on the client side, Zuul acts as an **API gateway** that routes incoming requests to appropriate microservices based on routing rules.

How Zuul Works:

- **Zuul Proxy**: It acts as the entry point for all incoming requests and is responsible for forwarding requests to appropriate microservices.

- **Routing**: Zuul handles dynamic routing and load balancing, distributing requests across available microservice instances.
- **Filters**: Zuul allows the creation of custom filters that can be used for tasks like authentication, logging, rate limiting, etc.

Setting Up Zuul for Routing and Load Balancing:

1. **Add Zuul and Eureka Dependencies**:
   o In your API Gateway application, include the dependencies for **Zuul** and **Eureka**.
2. **Enable Zuul Proxy**:
   o Use @EnableZuulProxy to enable Zuul as a proxy in your Spring Boot application.

```java
@SpringBootApplication
@EnableZuulProxy
public class ApiGatewayApplication {
    public static void main(String[] args) {

SpringApplication.run(ApiGatewayApplication.class, args);
    }
}
```

127

3. **Configure   Routing   with   Zuul**
    (`application.properties` or `application.yml`):
    You can configure routing rules for Zuul by specifying
    the microservice names and the corresponding endpoints.

```properties
zuul.routes.product-service.path=/products/**
zuul.routes.order-service.path=/orders/**
zuul.routes.payment-service.path=/payments/**
```

In this example:

- Requests starting with `/products/**` are forwarded to
  the **product-service**.
- Requests starting with `/orders/**` are forwarded to the
  order-service.
- Requests starting with `/payments/**` are forwarded to
  the **payment-service**.

Load Balancing in Zuul:

- Zuul uses **Ribbon** under the hood to load balance requests
  to the services. When a request arrives at Zuul, it queries
  Eureka for the available instances of the requested service
  and routes the request accordingly.

Summary

In this chapter, we explored the essential patterns of **service discovery** and **load balancing** in a microservices architecture.

- **Service Discovery** is managed with **Eureka**, allowing services to dynamically register and discover other services. This ensures that microservices can communicate with each other even as they scale up or down.
- **Client-Side Load Balancing** is handled by **Ribbon**, which enables services to distribute requests among available service instances, ensuring efficient use of resources and preventing bottlenecks.
- **Server-Side Load Balancing** is managed by **Zuul**, which acts as an API gateway to route and load balance incoming requests to microservices.

By leveraging **Eureka**, **Ribbon**, and **Zuul**, you can build a resilient, scalable microservices architecture where services can dynamically discover each other, and requests are efficiently distributed across service instances. In the following chapters, we will continue to explore how to enhance the reliability and scalability of your microservices system.

CHAPTER 12

MICROSERVICES RESILIENCE WITH HYSTRIX

In this chapter, we will explore how to make your microservices more **resilient** by using the **Circuit Breaker** pattern and the **Hystrix** library. Microservices rely on many interdependent services, and when one service fails, it can trigger a cascade of failures across the entire system. To mitigate this risk, the **Circuit Breaker** pattern can be applied to prevent such cascading failures and enhance the fault tolerance of your microservices.

Introduction to the Circuit Breaker Pattern

The **Circuit Breaker pattern** is a design pattern used to handle failures in distributed systems, specifically in a **microservices architecture**. The idea is inspired by the **electrical circuit breaker**, which disconnects a failing circuit to prevent damage to the system.

In microservices, services often rely on each other, and a failure in one service can cause other services to fail as well, potentially bringing down the entire system. The **Circuit Breaker** pattern helps by **detecting failures early** and temporarily stopping requests to a failing service, allowing the system to continue operating without full breakdowns. When the service recovers, the circuit breaker allows requests to flow again.

The Circuit Breaker pattern typically has three states:

1. **Closed**: The circuit is working normally. Requests flow through to the service.
2. **Open**: The circuit is "broken" due to failures. Requests are **not forwarded** to the failing service, and an **error response** is returned immediately.
3. **Half-Open**: The circuit is partially open, and the system checks whether the service has recovered. A limited number of requests are allowed to test if the service is healthy again.

Why is the Circuit Breaker pattern necessary?

- In a **microservices architecture**, services are dependent on each other, so failures in one service can trigger failures in other services.
- Without a circuit breaker, a small issue in one service could cause **cascading failures** across the entire system, leading to downtime or degraded performance.
- The Circuit Breaker pattern helps by **isolating failures**, allowing the system to continue running and recover quickly.

Using Hystrix for Fault Tolerance in Microservices

Hystrix is a library developed by **Netflix** to implement the **Circuit Breaker pattern** in Java applications. It provides a way to isolate failures in microservices and prevent cascading failures by automatically handling errors, timeouts, and retries.

Hystrix works by wrapping potentially **failing operations** (such as HTTP requests to another microservice, database queries, etc.) in **command objects**. These commands are monitored for failures, and if a threshold is reached (e.g., if a service fails too many times), Hystrix will trigger the **circuit breaker** and stop further requests to that service.

Key Features of Hystrix:

1. **Circuit Breaker**: Automatically trips the circuit breaker when a service is failing or responding too slowly.
2. **Timeouts**: If a service doesn't respond within a set time, Hystrix will stop waiting and return an error or fallback response.
3. **Fallback**: You can define a fallback method that will be invoked when a service fails, allowing the system to return a default response instead of failing completely.
4. **Isolation**: Hystrix isolates services from each other, preventing a failure in one service from affecting others.

Example: Handling Failures in a Service with Hystrix

Let's go through an example of how to use **Hystrix** for fault tolerance in a microservice that calls an external **Product Service** to retrieve product details.

Step 1: Add Hystrix Dependency To use Hystrix in your Spring Boot application, you need to add the `spring-cloud-starter-netflix-hystrix` dependency in your `pom.xml` (for Maven).

xml

```xml
<dependency>

<groupId>org.springframework.cloud</groupId>
    <artifactId>spring-cloud-starter-netflix-hystrix</artifactId>
</dependency>
```

Step 2: Enable Hystrix in Your Application

To enable Hystrix, you need to annotate your main application class with `@EnableCircuitBreaker`:

java

```java
@SpringBootApplication
@EnableCircuitBreaker
```

133

```
public class ProductServiceApplication {
    public static void main(String[] args) {

SpringApplication.run(ProductServiceApplication
.class, args);
    }
}
```

This annotation tells Spring to scan for Hystrix commands and to enable circuit breaking in the application.

Step 3: Implementing a Service Call with Hystrix Command

Now, let's create a service that makes an HTTP call to another microservice to fetch product details. We will use **Hystrix** to handle failures and implement a **circuit breaker** for this service call.

Here's an example where we use @HystrixCommand to wrap the call to an external service:

```java
import
com.netflix.hystrix.contrib.javanica.annotation
.HystrixCommand;
import org.springframework.stereotype.Service;
import
org.springframework.web.client.RestTemplate;
```

```java
@Service
public class ProductService {

    private final RestTemplate restTemplate;

    public         ProductService(RestTemplate
restTemplate) {
        this.restTemplate = restTemplate;
    }

    @HystrixCommand(fallbackMethod        =
"fallbackProductDetails")
    public    String    getProductDetails(Long
productId) {
        // Simulating  a  service  call  to  get
product details from another microservice
        String            url            =
"http://localhost:8081/products/" + productId;
        return    restTemplate.getForObject(url,
String.class);
    }

    // Fallback method when the service fails
    public  String  fallbackProductDetails(Long
productId) {
        return "Product details are temporarily
unavailable. Please try again later.";
    }
```

```
}
```

Explanation:

- The `getProductDetails` method is wrapped with `@HystrixCommand`. If the external **Product Service** fails or is too slow, Hystrix will trigger the `fallbackProductDetails` method.
- The `fallbackProductDetails` method provides a fallback response when the service fails, ensuring that the application continues functioning despite the failure.

Step 4: Handling Timeouts and Circuit Breaker Configuration

You can configure Hystrix for timeouts, circuit breaking thresholds, and more. The following configuration can be added to the `application.properties` or `application.yml` to control Hystrix behavior.

properties

```
hystrix.command.default.execution.isolation.thr
ead.timeoutInMilliseconds=3000
hystrix.command.default.circuitBreaker.requestV
olumeThreshold=10
hystrix.command.default.circuitBreaker.sleepWin
dowInMilliseconds=5000
```

```
hystrix.command.default.circuitBreaker.errorThr
esholdPercentage=50
```

Explanation of Configuration:

- `timeoutInMilliseconds`: Sets the timeout for service calls in milliseconds (e.g., 3 seconds).
- `requestVolumeThreshold`: The minimum number of requests to track before the circuit breaker will open if the error rate is high (e.g., 10 requests).
- `sleepWindowInMilliseconds`: Defines how long to wait before checking if the service has recovered after the circuit is open (e.g., 5 seconds).
- `errorThresholdPercentage`: The percentage of failed requests that will trigger the circuit breaker to open (e.g., 50%).

Monitoring Hystrix Dashboard

Hystrix provides a **dashboard** to monitor the health of your services in real-time. The Hystrix dashboard displays metrics such as the number of requests, success and failure rates, and circuit breaker status for each command.

To enable the **Hystrix Dashboard**, add the `spring-cloud-starter-netflix-hystrix-dashboard` dependency to your project:

xml

```
<dependency>

<groupId>org.springframework.cloud</groupId>
    <artifactId>spring-cloud-starter-netflix-
hystrix-dashboard</artifactId>
</dependency>
```

Then, enable the dashboard in your main application class:

java

```
@SpringBootApplication
@EnableCircuitBreaker
@EnableHystrixDashboard
public class ProductServiceApplication {
    public static void main(String[] args) {

SpringApplication.run(ProductServiceApplication
.class, args);
    }
}
```

The Hystrix Dashboard will be accessible at http://localhost:8080/hystrix to view real-time metrics of the circuit breakers and the health of your services.

Summary

In this chapter, we've introduced the **Circuit Breaker pattern** and explored how **Hystrix** can be used to implement fault tolerance and resilience in your microservices architecture. By using Hystrix, we can prevent cascading failures, isolate services, and provide fallback methods in case of errors.

We walked through an example where we used **Hystrix** to create a **ProductService** that calls an external microservice and handles failures with a fallback response. Additionally, we covered how to configure **timeouts**, **circuit breaker thresholds**, and how to monitor your services using the **Hystrix Dashboard**.

By implementing Hystrix in your microservices, you can enhance the **resilience** of your system, ensuring that even if one service fails, the entire system remains functional and responsive. In the next chapters, we will explore more advanced topics in microservices, including **distributed tracing** and **health checks** to further improve the reliability of your system.

CHAPTER 13

DEPLOYING MICROSERVICES WITH DOCKER

In this chapter, we will explore **Docker** and its role in **containerizing microservices**. Docker is a powerful platform for building, shipping, and running applications in isolated environments called **containers**. By using Docker, you can package your **Java-based microservices** into self-contained, lightweight containers that can be run on any environment, ensuring consistency across development, testing, and production.

We will cover the basics of containerization with Docker, show you how to create Docker images for your Java microservices, and walk through a **real-world deployment example** using **Docker Compose** to deploy multiple microservices.

Introduction to Containerization with Docker

What is Docker? Docker is a platform for **containerization**, which involves packaging an application and all its dependencies (libraries, environment variables, configurations, etc.) into a **container**. Containers provide an isolated and consistent environment for running applications, ensuring that they run the same way regardless of the underlying infrastructure.

- **Docker Images**: A Docker image is a blueprint or template that defines the environment and the application. It contains the application code, libraries, dependencies, and configuration files.
- **Docker Containers**: A Docker container is a running instance of a Docker image. It is lightweight, isolated, and portable.
- **Docker Hub**: A cloud-based registry where you can find, store, and share Docker images.

Why Use Docker for Microservices?

- **Portability**: Docker containers can run on any machine, whether it's a developer's laptop, a staging server, or a production environment in the cloud.
- **Isolation**: Each microservice runs in its own container, which ensures that they do not interfere with each other. This isolation makes it easier to manage, update, and scale microservices independently.
- **Consistency**: Docker ensures that your microservices will run the same way across different environments, eliminating the "it works on my machine" problem.

- **Scalability**: Docker enables easy scaling of microservices by running multiple containers of the same service, all while being managed efficiently.

How to Create Docker Images for Java-Based Microservices

To containerize a **Java-based microservice**, you need to create a **Dockerfile**, which defines how to build the Docker image for your service.

Step 1: Create a Dockerfile The Dockerfile is a script that contains instructions for building a Docker image. It specifies the base image to use, copies the application code, installs dependencies, and defines how the application will run inside the container.

Here's an example of a **Dockerfile** for a Spring Boot-based microservice:

```
Dockerfile

# Step 1: Use an official OpenJDK base image
FROM openjdk:11-jre-slim

# Step 2: Set the working directory inside the container
WORKDIR /app
```

```
# Step 3:    the compiled JAR file into the
container
 target/product-service.jar        /app/product-
service.jar


# Step 4: Expose the port the app will run on
EXPOSE 8080


# Step 5: Define the command to run the app
ENTRYPOINT   ["java",   "-jar",   "/app/product-
service.jar"]
```

Explanation:

- `FROM openjdk:11-jre-slim`: We are using the official OpenJDK 11 image as the base image, which includes a Java runtime environment.
- `WORKDIR /app`: This sets the working directory inside the container.
- `target/product-service.jar /app/product-service.jar`: This copies the compiled JAR file (from your local `target` folder) into the container.
- `EXPOSE 8080`: This exposes port 8080, which is the port our Spring Boot microservice will run on.
- `ENTRYPOINT ["java", "-jar", "/app/product-service.jar"]`: This defines the command to run the application inside the container.

Step 2: Build the Docker Image Once the `Dockerfile` is created, you can build the Docker image using the following command in the project directory (where the `Dockerfile` is located):

bash

```
docker build -t product-service .
```

This command will build the Docker image and tag it as `product-service`. The . specifies that the build context is the current directory.

Step 3: Run the Docker Container After the image is built, you can run a container based on the image with the following command:

bash

```
docker run -d -p 8080:8080 --name product-service
product-service
```

- `-d`: Runs the container in detached mode.
- `-p 8080:8080`: Maps port 8080 on the host machine to port 8080 inside the container.
- `--name product-service`: Names the container `product-service`.

144

- `product-service`: This is the name of the image we built earlier.

You can now access the product service at `http://localhost:8080` in your browser or API testing tool.

Real-World Deployment Example with Docker Compose

While individual containers are great, managing multiple microservices can become complex. That's where **Docker Compose** comes in. Docker Compose allows you to define and run multi-container applications using a simple YAML file.

In a microservices architecture, you may have multiple services that need to interact with each other. For example, you may have a **product service**, an **order service**, and a **database service**. Docker Compose lets you define all these services and their dependencies in a single file and start them together with a single command.

Step 1: Create a `docker-compose.yml` File

Here's an example of a **docker-compose.yml** file that defines three services: `product-service`, `order-service`, and a database (`postgres`):

yaml

```yaml
version: '3.8'

services:
  product-service:
    image: product-service
    build: ./product-service
    ports:
      - "8080:8080"
    depends_on:
      - postgres

  order-service:
    image: order-service
    build: ./order-service
    ports:
      - "8081:8081"
    depends_on:
      - postgres

  postgres:
    image: postgres:13
    environment:
      POSTGRES_USER: admin
      POSTGRES_PASSWORD: password
      POSTGRES_DB: orderdb
    volumes:
      - postgres-data:/var/lib/postgresql/data
    ports:
```

```
  - "5432:5432"

volumes:
  postgres-data:
```

Explanation:

- `product-service`, `order-service`: These are the names of the microservices in the application. Each service is defined with a specific image, and we specify the build context (e.g., `./product-service`).
- `depends_on`: This ensures that the database service (`postgres`) starts before the microservices.
- `postgres`: This defines the PostgreSQL database service, using the official `postgres` image. It also sets up the environment variables for the PostgreSQL user, password, and database name.
- `volumes`: This ensures persistent storage for the PostgreSQL database data.

Step 2: Build and Run the Containers with Docker Compose

To build and start the services defined in the `docker-compose.yml` file, run the following command:

```bash
docker-compose up --build
```

- `--build`: This flag ensures that Docker Compose rebuilds the images if there are any changes to the services' Dockerfiles.

This command will download the necessary Docker images (if they're not already present), build the services, and start the containers. You can now access the services as follows:

- **Product Service**: `http://localhost:8080`
- **Order Service**: `http://localhost:8081`
- **PostgreSQL**: Accessible on port `5432`.

Step 3: Stopping and Removing Containers

To stop and remove all running containers, you can use:

bash

```
docker-compose down
```

This will stop and remove the containers, networks, and volumes created by `docker-compose up`.

Summary

In this chapter, we covered how to **containerize Java-based microservices** using **Docker**. We learned how to create Docker images using a `Dockerfile`, how to run those images as containers, and how Docker Compose helps manage and deploy multiple microservices with ease.

Key takeaways from this chapter:

- **Containerization** ensures that each microservice is isolated, portable, and runs consistently across different environments.
- **Docker Compose** allows you to define and manage multi-container applications, making it easier to deploy complex systems with multiple microservices and dependencies.
- By using Docker for deploying microservices, you can ensure greater **scalability**, **portability**, and **resilience** in your microservices architecture.

In the next chapters, we will explore how to scale and secure these Dockerized microservices and integrate them into a complete, production-ready system.

CHAPTER 14

KUBERNETES: ORCHESTRATING MICROSERVICES AT SCALE

In this chapter, we will dive into **Kubernetes**, the leading platform for **container orchestration**. Kubernetes helps you automate the deployment, scaling, and management of containerized applications, such as microservices. We will explore how Kubernetes can be used to deploy microservices in clusters, how to scale them efficiently, and how Kubernetes simplifies managing microservices at scale.

Introduction to Kubernetes for Container Orchestration

What is Kubernetes? Kubernetes (often abbreviated as **K8s**) is an open-source platform for automating the deployment, scaling, and operation of containerized applications. Kubernetes was originally developed by **Google** and has since become the industry standard for container orchestration.

Kubernetes addresses the complexity of managing microservices at scale by providing a platform for:

- **Automating the deployment** of containers.

- **Scaling** services up or down based on demand.
- **Managing the lifecycle** of containers, ensuring that they are running as expected.
- **Handling networking** between containers and microservices.
- **Providing self-healing capabilities**, such as automatic restarts and load balancing.

Why Kubernetes for Microservices? As microservices architectures grow, managing a large number of containers and services can become increasingly complex. Kubernetes abstracts away the complexity of managing and orchestrating containers, enabling organizations to focus on developing their applications. Some key benefits of using Kubernetes in a microservices architecture include:

- **Declarative Configuration**: Kubernetes allows you to define how you want your services to run in configuration files, making it easier to manage and automate deployments.
- **Self-Healing**: Kubernetes can detect when a container or service is unhealthy and automatically restart or reschedule it to another node in the cluster.
- **Load Balancing and Service Discovery**: Kubernetes includes built-in load balancing, making it easier for services to discover and communicate with each other in a distributed system.

Deploying Microservices in Kubernetes Clusters

1. Kubernetes Architecture: Kubernetes works by deploying containers into a cluster of machines. The main components of the Kubernetes architecture are:

- **Nodes**: Physical or virtual machines that run the applications and workloads. Each node contains a **Kubelet**, which is an agent responsible for managing containers on that node.
- **Pods**: A **Pod** is the smallest deployable unit in Kubernetes. It represents one or more containers that are scheduled together on the same node and share the same network namespace, storage, and configuration.
- **Control Plane**: The control plane manages the overall state of the cluster. It includes components like the **API server**, **scheduler**, **controller manager**, and **etcd** (a distributed key-value store that holds the cluster's state).

2. Setting Up a Kubernetes Cluster: To deploy microservices in Kubernetes, you need a running Kubernetes cluster. There are several ways to set up a cluster:

- **Minikube**: A tool for running Kubernetes clusters locally for development and testing.

- **Cloud Providers**: Major cloud providers like **Google Cloud (GKE)**, **Amazon Web Services (EKS)**, and **Azure (AKS)** offer managed Kubernetes services.
- **Kubeadm**: A tool that helps set up a Kubernetes cluster on physical or virtual machines.

3. Deploying Microservices to Kubernetes:

Once your Kubernetes cluster is set up, you can begin deploying microservices. The deployment is typically done using **YAML files**, which define the configuration for the Kubernetes resources.

Here's an example of a Kubernetes deployment configuration for a **product-service** microservice:

yaml

```
apiVersion: apps/v1
kind: Deployment
metadata:
  name: product-service
spec:
  replicas: 3
  selector:
    matchLabels:
      app: product-service
  template:
    metadata:
      labels:
```

153

```
      app: product-service
spec:
  containers:
  - name: product-service
    image: product-service:latest
    ports:
    - containerPort: 8080
```

Explanation:

- `apiVersion: apps/v1`: Defines the version of the Kubernetes API used for deployments.

- `kind: Deployment`: Specifies that this is a **Deployment** resource, which manages the application's desired state (e.g., number of replicas, container images, etc.).

- `replicas: 3`: Specifies that 3 instances (replicas) of the product-service should be run.

- `containers`: Defines the container(s) to be run in the pod, specifying the Docker image to use (`product-service:latest`), and the port the container listens on.

To apply the deployment, save this YAML file as `product-service-deployment.yaml` and run:

`bash`

```
kubectl apply -f product-service-deployment.yaml
```

This will create a **Deployment** in Kubernetes, which will ensure that 3 instances of the **product-service** are running and managed by the system.

4. Exposing Microservices with Services:

To allow communication between microservices, Kubernetes uses **Services**. A Kubernetes **Service** defines a logical set of pods and a policy by which to access them. You can expose a service internally or externally, depending on your needs.

Here's an example of exposing the **product-service** as a **ClusterIP** service, which is accessible only within the cluster:

yaml

```
apiVersion: v1
kind: Service
metadata:
  name: product-service
spec:
  selector:
    app: product-service
  ports:
    - protocol: TCP
      port: 8080
      targetPort: 8080
  clusterIP: None  # This sets the service to be
accessed only within the cluster
```

To create this service, save the YAML as `product-service-service.yaml` and run:

```bash

kubectl apply -f product-service-service.yaml
```

Kubernetes will automatically create a DNS entry for the `product-service` that allows other services in the cluster to discover and communicate with it.

Scaling and Managing Microservices Using Kubernetes

1. Horizontal Scaling with Kubernetes:

One of the key advantages of Kubernetes is its ability to **scale microservices** dynamically. Kubernetes can automatically adjust the number of replicas of a microservice based on resource utilization (e.g., CPU, memory), or it can be manually scaled by adjusting the replica count in the deployment configuration.

To scale the **product-service** deployment to 5 replicas, run the following command:

```bash

kubectl scale deployment product-service --replicas=5
```

156

This command tells Kubernetes to run 5 instances of the **product-service**, ensuring that the service can handle more traffic and is highly available.

2. Auto-Scaling:

Kubernetes also supports **auto-scaling** through the **Horizontal Pod Autoscaler**. The Horizontal Pod Autoscaler adjusts the number of replicas based on CPU usage or custom metrics.

Here's an example of setting up auto-scaling for the **product-service**:

```bash
kubectl autoscale deployment product-service --cpu-percent=50 --min=1 --max=10
```

This command creates an autoscaler that will scale the **product-service** deployment between 1 and 10 replicas based on CPU usage, with a target CPU usage of 50%.

3. Rolling Updates and Rollbacks:

Kubernetes provides built-in support for **rolling updates**, which allow you to update your microservices without downtime. When you update the Docker image or configuration for a microservice, Kubernetes will gradually replace the old pods with new ones, ensuring that the service remains available during the update.

If something goes wrong during the update, you can easily **rollback** to the previous version of the deployment:

```bash
kubectl rollout undo deployment/product-service
```

This command rolls back to the last stable deployment of the **product-service**.

4. Health Checks:

Kubernetes allows you to define **liveness** and **readiness** probes to check if a microservice is running correctly and ready to accept traffic.

- **Liveness Probe**: Checks if the service is still alive and healthy.
- **Readiness Probe**: Checks if the service is ready to accept traffic (useful when the service is still starting).

Here's an example of adding health checks to a **product-service**:

```yaml
spec:
  containers:
  - name: product-service
    image: product-service:latest
```

158

```
ports:
- containerPort: 8080
livenessProbe:
  httpGet:
    path: /actuator/health
    port: 8080
  initialDelaySeconds: 10
  periodSeconds: 5
readinessProbe:
  httpGet:
    path: /actuator/health
    port: 8080
  initialDelaySeconds: 5
  periodSeconds: 5
```

This configuration uses the /actuator/health endpoint (provided by Spring Boot Actuator) to check the service's health.

Summary

In this chapter, we explored **Kubernetes**, the leading platform for **container orchestration**. We covered how Kubernetes helps manage and scale **microservices** in a cluster environment. Key topics included:

- **Kubernetes architecture**, including nodes, pods, and the control plane.

- **Deploying microservices in Kubernetes** using **YAML files** to define deployments and services.

- **Scaling microservices** horizontally by adjusting the number of replicas and using auto-scaling features.

- Managing **rolling updates** and **rollbacks** to ensure zero-downtime deployments.

- Configuring **health checks** to ensure that microservices are running and ready to accept traffic.

Kubernetes makes it easier to deploy and manage microservices at scale, providing powerful tools for scaling, rolling updates, fault tolerance, and service discovery. In the next chapters, we will explore additional features like **continuous deployment** and **security** for microservices running on Kubernetes.

CHAPTER 15

CI/CD FOR MICROSERVICES WITH JENKINS

In this chapter, we will explore **Continuous Integration (CI)** and **Continuous Delivery (CD)**, essential practices in modern software development. We will also guide you through setting up a **CI/CD pipeline** using **Jenkins**, an open-source automation server widely used for automating various aspects of software development. Finally, we will demonstrate how to deploy **Java-based microservices** automatically using Jenkins.

Introduction to Continuous Integration and Continuous Delivery

1. Continuous Integration (CI): Continuous Integration is the practice of automatically building and testing code every time a developer pushes changes to a version control system (e.g., Git). The main goal of CI is to ensure that code changes integrate seamlessly with the existing codebase, reducing integration problems and improving code quality.

Key benefits of CI:

- **Early detection of errors:** By automatically building and testing the code, developers can catch issues early, before they become problems.
- **Faster feedback:** Developers get immediate feedback about the quality of their changes, allowing them to make necessary adjustments quickly.
- **Improved collaboration:** CI encourages team collaboration by integrating changes from multiple developers frequently, making it easier to work together on the same project.

2. Continuous Delivery (CD): Continuous Delivery extends CI by automating the deployment of applications to production-like environments. With CD, every change that passes automated testing is automatically deployed to a staging environment or production. The key distinction between CI and CD is that while CI automates the integration of code, CD automates the deployment process.

Key benefits of CD:

- **Faster release cycles:** With automation, features and bug fixes can be deployed faster and more reliably to production.
- **Reduced risk of deployment issues:** By regularly deploying to staging environments, CD ensures that deployment issues are identified earlier in the process.

- **Improved quality assurance:** Frequent deployments to testing environments allow for comprehensive and continuous testing, improving overall quality.

Setting up a CI/CD Pipeline with Jenkins

1. Introduction to Jenkins: Jenkins is an open-source automation server used to automate various stages of the software development lifecycle, such as building, testing, and deploying applications. It integrates with popular version control systems (like Git), build tools (like Maven or Gradle), and deployment systems to create a **CI/CD pipeline**.

Key Jenkins Concepts:

- **Jenkins Jobs:** A job is a task or step in the CI/CD pipeline, such as building code or deploying an application.
- **Pipelines:** Jenkins pipelines define a series of steps, such as building, testing, and deploying, that are executed automatically when triggered by events like a code commit.
- **Plugins:** Jenkins supports a wide range of plugins that integrate with other tools (e.g., Git, Maven, Docker, Kubernetes) to extend its functionality.

2. Installing Jenkins: To get started with Jenkins, you need to install it on a server or use a cloud-based Jenkins service (such as **Jenkins X** or **CloudBees**).

- **Installing Jenkins Locally (via Docker):** Jenkins can be installed as a Docker container for ease of setup. You can run the following command to pull and run the latest Jenkins image:

bash

```
docker pull jenkins/jenkins:lts
docker run -d -p 8080:8080 -p 50000:50000 --name
jenkins jenkins/jenkins:lts
```

Once Jenkins is running, navigate to `http://localhost:8080` in your browser to complete the initial setup, including unlocking Jenkins and installing recommended plugins.

- **Installing Jenkins on Ubuntu (alternative method):**

  bash

```
sudo apt update
sudo apt install openjdk-11-jdk
sudo apt install jenkins
sudo systemctl start jenkins
```

164

After installation, access Jenkins at `http://localhost:8080` and complete the setup process.

3. Setting Up Jenkins for CI/CD:

Now that Jenkins is up and running, let's set up a simple **CI/CD pipeline** for a **Java-based microservice**.

Step 1: Create a New Jenkins Job (Pipeline Job):

1. Log in to Jenkins and click on **New Item**.
2. Select **Pipeline** and provide a name (e.g., `ProductServicePipeline`).
3. Click **OK** to create the pipeline.

Step 2: Define the Pipeline in `Jenkinsfile`: Jenkins pipelines are typically defined in a file called **`Jenkinsfile`**, which contains the steps for the build, test, and deploy process. The `Jenkinsfile` is usually placed in the root directory of your project repository.

Here's an example `Jenkinsfile` for a Java-based microservice using Maven:

```groovy
pipeline {
    agent any
```

```
environment {
    MVN_HOME = '/usr/local/maven'  // Define
Maven home if needed
    }

    stages {
        stage('Checkout') {
            steps {
                // Checkout the code from Git
                git    'https://github.com/your-
repo/product-service.git'
            }
        }

        stage('Build') {
            steps {
                // Build the project using Maven
                sh  "'$MVN_HOME/bin/mvn'  clean
install"
            }
        }

        stage('Test') {
            steps {
                // Run tests (JUnit tests, etc.)
                sh "'$MVN_HOME/bin/mvn' test"
            }
        }
```

```
stage('Dockerize') {
    steps {
        // Build Docker image
        sh 'docker build -t product-
service .'
    }
}

stage('Deploy to Staging') {
    steps {
        // Deploy the application to
staging (could be Kubernetes, Docker Compose,
etc.)
        sh 'docker-compose -f docker-
compose-staging.yml up -d'
    }
}

stage('Deploy to Production') {
    steps {
        // Deploy the application to
production (optional for staging setup)
        input 'Deploy to Production?'
        sh 'docker-compose -f docker-
compose-prod.yml up -d'
    }
}
}
```

167

```
post {
    success {
        echo        'Pipeline        successfully
completed!'
    }
    failure {
        echo 'Pipeline failed!'
    }
}
}
```

Explanation:

- **Checkout Stage:** This stage pulls the latest code from the Git repository.
- **Build Stage:** This compiles the Java application using **Maven**.
- **Test Stage:** This runs unit tests (e.g., using **JUnit**).
- **Dockerize Stage:** This builds a Docker image for the microservice.
- **Deploy to Staging and Deploy to Production Stages:** These stages deploy the application using **Docker Compose** to either a **staging** or **production** environment.

Step 3: Run the Jenkins Pipeline: Once the `Jenkinsfile` is added to your repository and configured in Jenkins:

1. Go to the **Pipeline** job you created in Jenkins.

2. Click **Build Now** to start the CI/CD pipeline. Jenkins will automatically execute each stage defined in the pipeline, including building, testing, and deploying the microservice.

Deploying Java Microservices Automatically via Jenkins

With the Jenkins pipeline in place, the deployment of Java-based microservices becomes automated. Let's break down the steps for deploying the microservice automatically using Jenkins and Docker.

Step 1: Build Docker Images Automatically: Every time a change is pushed to the Git repository, Jenkins will:

1. **Checkout** the code.
2. **Build** the Java microservice using Maven.
3. **Test** the service (e.g., with JUnit tests).
4. **Dockerize** the service by building a Docker image for it.

The `Dockerfile` for the microservice (shown in a previous chapter) should already be in the project repository, allowing Jenkins to build it during the pipeline process.

Step 2: Deploy to Staging: Jenkins will deploy the newly built Docker image to a **staging environment** (which could be Docker Compose, Kubernetes, or any other platform you choose).

In the **staging deployment stage**, the Jenkins pipeline uses `docker-compose` to start up the service in a **staging environment**.

Step 3: Deploy to Production: Once the service is verified in the staging environment, Jenkins can automatically deploy it to **production**. The `Deploy to Production` stage in the `Jenkinsfile` can be set to require manual approval (`input 'Deploy to Production?'`) to ensure that you only deploy to production when you're ready.

Summary

In this chapter, we explored the concepts of **Continuous Integration (CI)** and **Continuous Delivery (CD)** and how Jenkins can be used to automate the deployment pipeline for **Java-based microservices**.

Key points from this chapter:

- **CI/CD** practices improve development speed and quality by automating the process of building, testing, and deploying applications.
- We set up a Jenkins pipeline that automates the entire CI/CD process for a **Java microservice**, including

170

building the microservice with Maven, testing it, creating Docker images, and deploying the service.

- **Docker Compose** was used to deploy the microservice to staging and production environments.

Jenkins makes it easier to integrate all aspects of the **CI/CD pipeline**, allowing you to quickly deploy updates to your microservices and keep your system running smoothly. As we continue to explore microservices, we will cover more advanced deployment strategies, including **rolling updates** and **blue-green deployments**.

CHAPTER 16

MONITORING AND LOGGING IN MICROSERVICES

In this chapter, we will explore the **importance of monitoring** and **logging** in a **microservices environment**. As microservices architectures become more complex, with multiple services running independently, it becomes increasingly important to have tools in place to monitor performance, track issues, and maintain the health of the system. We will look at some of the most widely used tools for monitoring and logging in microservices, including **Spring Boot Actuator**, the **ELK Stack**, **Prometheus**, and **Grafana**. Finally, we will walk through a **real-world example** of setting up monitoring and logging for microservices.

Importance of Monitoring and Logging in a Microservices Environment

In a traditional monolithic application, all components reside in a single codebase and are often deployed together. This simplifies monitoring and logging, as the system is tightly integrated. However, in a **microservices architecture**, each microservice operates as an independent entity, often in separate containers or

172

virtual machines, making it harder to get a clear overview of the system's performance and behavior.

Why is monitoring important in microservices?

- **Visibility into Service Health**: Monitoring helps you understand how each microservice is performing and whether it's meeting the expected service levels.
- **Detecting Failures**: Early detection of failures (e.g., service downtime, high error rates) enables teams to address issues before they affect customers.
- **Scaling**: By monitoring resource usage (e.g., CPU, memory), you can automatically scale microservices up or down based on demand.
- **Performance Optimization**: Monitoring helps identify bottlenecks, slow responses, or inefficient processes, allowing teams to optimize their microservices for better performance.

Why is logging important in microservices?

- **Debugging and Troubleshooting**: Microservices are distributed systems, so tracking down issues can be difficult. Logs help trace the execution of requests across various services, providing insights into the cause of failures.

- **Audit Trails**: Logs provide an audit trail that records the flow of requests and changes in the system, which is useful for security and regulatory compliance.
- **Distributed Tracing**: Logs help track how requests flow through various microservices, which is crucial for troubleshooting performance or errors in a distributed system.

Tools for Monitoring and Logging

Let's review some of the most commonly used tools for monitoring and logging in a microservices architecture.

1. Spring Boot Actuator:

Spring Boot Actuator is a library that provides built-in functionality for monitoring and managing Spring Boot applications. It offers several **endpoints** that give insights into the health, metrics, environment, and various other details of a Spring Boot application.

- **Health Checks**: Spring Boot Actuator includes a health check endpoint (`/actuator/health`) that checks the status of various system components (e.g., database, disk space, etc.).

174

- **Metrics**: Actuator provides a `/actuator/metrics` endpoint to monitor key performance metrics (e.g., memory usage, garbage collection statistics).

- **Environment Information**: The `/actuator/env` endpoint provides information about the environment, including properties and configurations.

How to Set Up Spring Boot Actuator:

1. Add the `spring-boot-starter-actuator` dependency to your project:

xml

```
<dependency>

<groupId>org.springframework.boot</groupId>
    <artifactId>spring-boot-starter-actuator</artifactId>
</dependency>
```

2. Enable and customize the endpoints in the `application.properties` or `application.yml` file:

properties

```
management.endpoints.web.exposure.include
=health,metrics,info
management.endpoint.health.show-
details=always
```

3. Access the actuator endpoints, such as:
    o   `http://localhost:8080/actuator/heal
        th` (shows service health)
    o   `http://localhost:8080/actuator/metr
        ics` (shows performance metrics)

2. ELK Stack (Elasticsearch, Logstash, Kibana):

The **ELK Stack** is a powerful toolset for **logging** and **searching** logs in microservices environments.

*   **Elasticsearch**: A distributed search and analytics engine that stores logs and makes them searchable in real-time.
*   **Logstash**: A tool for **collecting**, **parsing**, and **transforming** logs from various sources, including microservices. It then forwards these logs to **Elasticsearch**.
*   **Kibana**: A visualization tool that allows you to explore and visualize logs stored in **Elasticsearch** through a web interface.

How the ELK Stack Works:

*   Microservices produce logs that are sent to **Logstash**.

176

- **Logstash** processes and forwards the logs to **Elasticsearch** for indexing and storage.
- **Kibana** provides an intuitive interface to search and visualize the logs.

Setting Up the ELK Stack:

1. **Install Elasticsearch** and **Kibana** on a server or use a managed service like **Elastic Cloud**.
2. **Install Logstash** and configure it to pull logs from your microservices (e.g., using Filebeat or Docker logging drivers).
3. Configure your microservices to send logs in a structured format (JSON) that Logstash can process.

3. Prometheus and Grafana:

Prometheus is an open-source monitoring and alerting toolkit designed for **containerized applications** and **microservices**. It pulls metrics from various sources (including **Spring Boot Actuator**) and stores them in a time-series database. **Grafana** is used for visualizing these metrics in dashboards.

- **Prometheus** collects metrics from microservices via **HTTP endpoints**.
- **Grafana** is used to create visual dashboards that display metrics like CPU usage, memory consumption, and request latencies.

Setting Up Prometheus and Grafana:

1. **Install Prometheus** and configure it to scrape metrics from your microservices (using `actuator/prometheus` endpoints).

   Example `prometheus.yml` configuration:

   ```yaml
   scrape_configs:
     - job_name: 'spring-boot-app'
       metrics_path: '/actuator/prometheus'
       static_configs:
         - targets: ['localhost:8080']
   ```

2. **Install Grafana** and configure it to connect to Prometheus as a data source.
3. Create **Grafana dashboards** to visualize metrics such as response times, error rates, and request counts.

Prometheus Example: You can use **Spring Boot Actuator** to expose Prometheus-compatible metrics by adding the `micrometer-registry-prometheus` dependency:

```xml
<dependency>
    <groupId>io.micrometer</groupId>
```

```
<artifactId>micrometer-registry-
prometheus</artifactId>
</dependency>
```

Once this is set up, you can access the metrics at `/actuator/prometheus` and have Prometheus scrape them.

Real-World Example: Setting up Logging and Monitoring for Microservices

Let's walk through a **real-world example** of setting up monitoring and logging for a **microservices-based e-commerce platform** using **Spring Boot Actuator**, the **ELK Stack**, and **Prometheus & Grafana**.

Step 1: Enable Spring Boot Actuator for Metrics and Health

- Add the `spring-boot-starter-actuator` dependency to the `product-service` and `order-service` microservices.
- In the `application.properties`, expose the `/actuator/health` and `/actuator/metrics` endpoints for monitoring.

Step 2: Set Up the ELK Stack for Logging

- **Elasticsearch**: Set up Elasticsearch to index and store logs from your microservices.
- **Logstash**: Install and configure Logstash to collect logs from **Docker containers** running the microservices and send them to Elasticsearch.
- **Kibana**: Use Kibana to visualize and analyze logs, helping to trace issues like failed orders or service downtimes.

Logstash Configuration Example:

```plaintext
plaintext

input {
  file {
    path => "/var/log/product-service.log"
    start_position => "beginning"
  }
}

output {
  elasticsearch {
    hosts => ["http://localhost:9200"]
    index => "microservice-logs"
  }
}
```

Step 3: Set Up Prometheus and Grafana for Metrics

- Install **Prometheus** to scrape metrics from the `product-service` and `order-service` at `/actuator/prometheus`.
- Install **Grafana** to visualize metrics like response times, error rates, and service availability.

Prometheus Configuration Example:

yaml

```yaml
scrape_configs:
  - job_name: 'product-service'
    metrics_path: '/actuator/prometheus'
    static_configs:
      - targets: ['localhost:8080']
  - job_name: 'order-service'
    metrics_path: '/actuator/prometheus'
    static_configs:
      - targets: ['localhost:8081']
```

Once Prometheus is set up, it will start collecting metrics from the exposed `/actuator/prometheus` endpoints of both services. These metrics can then be visualized in **Grafana** dashboards.

Grafana Dashboard Example: Create a dashboard that shows the **request count**, **error rate**, and **average response time** for the `product-service` and `order-service`. Set up **alerts** in

Grafana to notify you if response times exceed a certain threshold or if there are errors above a specific rate.

Summary

In this chapter, we explored the importance of **monitoring** and **logging** in microservices. As microservices become more distributed and complex, it's crucial to have the right tools in place to monitor their health, track performance metrics, and debug issues effectively.

Key takeaways:

- **Spring Boot Actuator** provides built-in support for exposing health and metrics endpoints for monitoring microservices.
- The **ELK Stack** (Elasticsearch, Logstash, Kibana) is a powerful tool for centralized logging and visualization of logs from multiple microservices.
- **Prometheus and Grafana** offer real-time monitoring and visualization of application metrics, making it easier to track service performance and set up alerts.

By setting up these tools, you can gain deep insights into your microservices' behavior and health, helping you quickly identify and address issues. In the following chapters, we will continue to explore **advanced monitoring** techniques and strategies for **observability** in microservices.

CHAPTER 17

TESTING MICROSERVICES

In this chapter, we will explore the different types of **testing** in the context of **microservices**. As microservices are independent services that communicate over a network, ensuring their correctness through testing is crucial. We will cover **unit testing**, **integration testing**, and **end-to-end testing**, focusing on the tools and techniques for effectively testing microservices. We will also look at how to use **JUnit** and **Mockito** for unit testing, strategies for integration testing, and methods for simulating complete workflows in end-to-end tests.

Unit Testing with JUnit and Mockito

1. Unit Testing: Unit tests are the first line of defense for testing the functionality of individual components or methods in a microservice. A **unit test** focuses on testing a single unit of work, such as a method or a class, in isolation from the rest of the application. The goal is to ensure that each unit behaves correctly, handling both expected and unexpected inputs.

For **Java microservices**, the most commonly used framework for unit testing is **JUnit**, and **Mockito** is a popular tool for mocking dependencies in unit tests.

2. Setting Up JUnit for Unit Testing: JUnit is a testing framework used to write and run tests in Java. It allows you to define test methods, group them into test suites, and check for expected results. JUnit 5 is the latest version and provides more powerful features for writing and organizing tests.

Adding JUnit Dependency: Add the following dependencies to your **pom.xml** file to use **JUnit** and **Mockito** in your project:

xml

```xml
<dependency>
    <groupId>org.junit.jupiter</groupId>
    <artifactId>junit-jupiter-api</artifactId>
    <version>5.7.0</version>
    <scope>test</scope>
</dependency>
<dependency>
    <groupId>org.mockito</groupId>
    <artifactId>mockito-core</artifactId>
    <version>3.8.0</version>
    <scope>test</scope>
</dependency>
```

3. Writing Unit Tests with JUnit and Mockito:

185

Let's say we have a **ProductService** class that interacts with a **ProductRepository** to fetch product details. We'll write unit tests to test the **ProductService** independently, mocking the **ProductRepository**.

Example class to be tested (ProductService):

java

```java
@Service
public class ProductService {

    private final ProductRepository productRepository;

    @Autowired
    public ProductService(ProductRepository productRepository) {
        this.productRepository = productRepository;
    }

    public Product getProductById(Long id) {
        return productRepository.findById(id)
            .orElseThrow(() -> new ProductNotFoundException("Product not found"));
    }
}
```

In this example, we will **mock** the `ProductRepository` dependency so that the test only focuses on the **ProductService** logic.

Example unit test using **JUnit 5** and **Mockito**:

```java
import static org.mockito.Mockito.*;
import                              static
org.junit.jupiter.api.Assertions.*;

import org.junit.jupiter.api.Test;
import org.mockito.*;

public class ProductServiceTest {

    @Mock
    private ProductRepository productRepository;

    @InjectMocks
    private ProductService productService;

    @Test
    public                                void
testGetProductById_whenProductExists() {
        // Arrange
        Product product = new Product(1L,
"Laptop", 1200.00);
```

187

```java
when(productRepository.findById(1L)).thenReturn
(Optional.of(product));

        // Act
        Product            result            =
productService.getProductById(1L);

        // Assert
        assertEquals("Laptop",
result.getName());
    }

    @Test
    public                            void
testGetProductById_whenProductNotFound() {
        // Arrange

when(productRepository.findById(1L)).thenReturn
(Optional.empty());

        // Act & Assert

assertThrows(ProductNotFoundException.class,  ()
-> productService.getProductById(1L));
    }
}
```

Explanation:

- `@Mock`: This annotation creates a mock instance of `ProductRepository` to simulate its behavior without involving an actual database.

- `@InjectMocks`: This annotation tells Mockito to inject the mocked `ProductRepository` into the `ProductService`.

- The `when(...).thenReturn(...)` pattern defines the mock behavior for methods in `ProductRepository`.

- We use **assertions** (`assertEquals`, `assertThrows`) to verify the expected results from the `ProductService`.

Integration Testing in Microservices

1. What is Integration Testing? Integration testing verifies that multiple components of the application work together as expected. In a microservices environment, this involves testing the interaction between services, databases, APIs, and other external systems.

While unit tests focus on individual components, integration tests ensure that the system as a whole functions correctly. For microservices, this typically means testing service communication, database interactions, and external APIs.

2. Setting Up Integration Tests with Spring Boot: Spring Boot provides excellent support for integration testing with annotations like @SpringBootTest, which loads the entire application context for testing.

Example Integration Test: Let's test the interaction between the **ProductService** and the **ProductRepository** by using an in-memory database for testing.

java

```java
@SpringBootTest
public class ProductServiceIntegrationTest {

    @Autowired
    private ProductService productService;

    @Autowired
    private ProductRepository productRepository;

    @Test
    public void testGetProductById_integration()
{
        // Arrange
        Product product = new Product(1L,
"Smartphone", 800.00);
        productRepository.save(product);

        // Act
        Product result =
productService.getProductById(1L);
```

```
    // Assert
    assertEquals("Smartphone",
result.getName());
    }
}
```

Explanation:

- @SpringBootTest: This annotation tells Spring Boot to load the entire application context, including the database.
- We save a product into the **in-memory database** and then test if the ProductService correctly retrieves the product using the ProductRepository.

3. Using Testcontainers for External Dependencies: For integration testing involving external systems (e.g., databases, message brokers), you can use **Testcontainers**, a Java library that allows you to spin up Docker containers for integration tests.

Example of using Testcontainers for a PostgreSQL database:

java

```
@Testcontainers
public class ProductServiceDatabaseTest {

    @Container
```

```java
public              PostgreSQLContainer<?>
postgresContainer            =            new
PostgreSQLContainer<>("postgres:13")
            .withDatabaseName("testdb")
            .withUsername("user")
            .withPassword("password");

    @Autowired
    private ProductRepository productRepository;

    @Test
    public void testSaveProduct_inDatabase() {
        // Arrange
        Product product = new Product(1L,
"Laptop", 1200.00);

        // Act
        productRepository.save(product);

        // Assert
        Product            result            =
productRepository.findById(1L).orElseThrow();
        assertEquals("Laptop",
result.getName());
    }
}
```

Explanation:

- **Testcontainers** allows you to run a **PostgreSQL container** in a test environment, ensuring that tests involving the database do not require a pre-existing database instance.
- This ensures a clean, isolated environment for integration tests.

End-to-End Testing: Simulating Entire Workflows

1. What is End-to-End Testing? End-to-end (E2E) testing verifies that the entire system, including multiple microservices and external systems, works as expected in a real-world scenario. In a microservices architecture, E2E testing simulates **user workflows** across different services to ensure everything is integrated properly.

E2E tests typically involve:

- **Simulating real user actions** across multiple services.
- **Testing the flow of data** between services (e.g., placing an order, payment processing).
- **Validating the system's response** (e.g., correct information is displayed, orders are processed).

2. Tools for E2E Testing: There are various tools for E2E testing:

- **Cucumber**: A tool for writing **behavior-driven tests** in plain language.
- **Selenium**: A framework for automating web browsers for testing user interfaces.
- **Postman/Newman**: Used for testing APIs and workflows by simulating HTTP requests.

3. Example: Using Postman for E2E API Testing:

You can use **Postman** to simulate end-to-end workflows by testing the flow between the **Product Service** and the **Order Service**.

Steps:

1. Create a collection in **Postman** to test the entire checkout process:
   - **Step 1**: Call the `/products/{id}` API to get product details.
   - **Step 2**: Use the product details to create an order via the `/orders` API.
   - **Step 3**: Verify that the order was created successfully.
2. Export the collection and use **Newman** (Postman's command-line tool) to automate the tests:

```bash
```

```
newman run checkout-workflow.json
```

Explanation:

- This approach allows you to simulate a complete user journey (e.g., browsing products, placing an order) across multiple microservices, ensuring that the full system works together.

Summary

In this chapter, we explored the different types of testing essential for **microservices**:

- **Unit testing** with **JUnit** and **Mockito** ensures that individual components of the system work correctly.
- **Integration testing** ensures that services communicate correctly with each other and with external systems.
- **End-to-end testing** simulates user workflows across multiple microservices to ensure the entire system functions correctly.

By using these testing strategies, you can ensure that your microservices are reliable, resilient, and ready for production. In the next chapters, we will continue to explore best practices for

scalability, **security**, and **deployment** in microservices architectures.

CHAPTER 18

HANDLING DISTRIBUTED TRANSACTIONS

In this chapter, we will address the challenges of managing **transactions** in a **microservices** architecture, where each service typically manages its own database. We will discuss the **SAGA** pattern, which is a widely used approach for handling distributed transactions, and show how to implement it in **Java**. Finally, we will walk through a real-world example of managing a distributed transaction across multiple services.

Challenges of Transactions in Microservices

In a traditional **monolithic architecture**, managing transactions is relatively straightforward. All components of the application typically share the same database, making it easier to manage **ACID transactions** (Atomicity, Consistency, Isolation, Durability) in a single, centralized context. However, as we break down an application into **microservices**, each service tends to have its own database, which introduces several challenges:

1. Data Consistency: In a distributed system, ensuring that data remains consistent across multiple services is a complex challenge. If a service fails after it has made part of a transaction but before it has completed, the system could end up in an inconsistent state.

2. Distributed Transactions: A **distributed transaction** involves multiple services and databases. Unlike traditional databases that support a single, atomic transaction across all components, microservices require a different approach to managing transactions across independent services.

Traditional **ACID transactions** are not suitable for microservices due to their reliance on a **centralized database** and **two-phase commit protocols** that are difficult to implement in a distributed environment.

3. Network Failures and Fault Tolerance: In microservices, communication between services occurs over a network, which can be unreliable. Network failures can result in partial updates to databases, leading to data inconsistency across services.

To address these challenges, **distributed transaction management** strategies such as **SAGA** and **event-driven architectures** are used.

The SAGA Pattern and Implementing It in Java

The **SAGA pattern** is a well-known pattern for managing distributed transactions in microservices architectures. Instead of relying on a single, centralized transaction manager, the SAGA pattern breaks the transaction into a series of **local transactions** that are managed by each individual microservice.

Each local transaction performs its work and, if successful, triggers the next service to perform its local transaction. If any of the local transactions fail, the SAGA pattern defines **compensating actions** (or **rollback steps**) to undo the changes made by previous transactions, ensuring that the system remains in a consistent state.

There are two main types of SAGA execution:

1. **Choreography-based SAGA**: In this approach, each service involved in the transaction knows about the other services and coordinates the transaction flow by emitting events and listening for events from other services.
2. **Orchestration-based SAGA**: In this approach, a central **orchestrator** (a specific service) manages the flow of the distributed transaction and calls the individual services in the correct order.

Example: Managing a Distributed Transaction

Let's walk through a real-world example of managing a distributed transaction in an **e-commerce platform** using the SAGA pattern. In this scenario, we have the following services:

- **Order Service**: Responsible for creating orders.
- **Inventory Service**: Responsible for managing the inventory.
- **Payment Service**: Responsible for processing payments.

Each service will handle its own local transaction, and we will implement a SAGA to manage the distributed transaction.

Step 1: Define the SAGA Steps

In this example, the SAGA will follow these steps:

1. **Order Service** creates an order and then sends a message to the **Inventory Service** to reserve the product.
2. **Inventory Service** reserves the product and then sends a message to the **Payment Service** to process the payment.
3. **Payment Service** processes the payment and, if successful, confirms the transaction to the **Order Service**.

If any step fails, a compensating action will be triggered:

- If payment fails, the **Inventory Service** will release the reserved product.
- If inventory reservation fails, the **Order Service** will cancel the order.

Step 2: Implementing the SAGA with Event-Driven Communication

To implement the SAGA pattern, we can use an **event-driven approach** where each service emits events to signal the completion of its local transaction. We can use **Kafka** or **RabbitMQ** as the event broker to manage communication between services.

Here's a basic example of how this might work in **Spring Boot** with **Kafka**.

Order Service (Producer):

java

```java
@Service
public class OrderService {

    @Autowired
    private KafkaTemplate<String, OrderEvent> kafkaTemplate;

    public void createOrder(Order order) {
```

```java
    // Step 1: Create the order
    orderRepository.save(order);

    // Step 2: Emit an event to Inventory
Service
    kafkaTemplate.send("inventory-topic",
new OrderCreatedEvent(order.getId()));
    }
}
```

Inventory Service (Consumer):

java

```java
@Service
public class InventoryService {

    @Autowired
    private                    KafkaTemplate<String,
InventoryEvent> kafkaTemplate;

    @KafkaListener(topics = "inventory-topic",
groupId = "inventory-group")
    public void reserveProduct(OrderCreatedEvent
event) {
        // Step 3: Reserve the product in
inventory
        boolean            success            =
inventoryRepository.reserveProduct(event.getOrd
erId());
```

```java
            if (success) {
                // Step 4: Emit an event to Payment
Service
                kafkaTemplate.send("payment-topic",
new ProductReservedEvent(event.getOrderId()));
            } else {
                // Compensating action: Notify Order
Service to cancel the order
                kafkaTemplate.send("order-topic",
new InventoryFailureEvent(event.getOrderId()));
            }
        }
}
```

Payment Service (Consumer):

```java
java

@Service
public class PaymentService {

    @Autowired
    private KafkaTemplate<String, PaymentEvent>
kafkaTemplate;

    @KafkaListener(topics    =    "payment-topic",
groupId = "payment-group")
    public                                    void
processPayment(ProductReservedEvent event) {
```

```java
        // Step 5: Process the payment
        boolean          success          =
paymentGateway.processPayment(event.getOrderId(
));

        if (success) {
            // Step 6: Emit a success event to
the Order Service
            kafkaTemplate.send("order-topic",
new PaymentSuccessEvent(event.getOrderId()));
        } else {
            // Compensating action:  Notify
Inventory Service to release the reserved product
            kafkaTemplate.send("inventory-
topic",                               new
PaymentFailureEvent(event.getOrderId()));
        }
    }
}
```

Order Service (Compensating Action):

```java
@Service
public class OrderService {

    @Autowired
    private  KafkaTemplate<String,  OrderEvent>
kafkaTemplate;
```

```java
@KafkaListener(topics    =    "order-topic",
groupId = "order-group")
    public                          void
handlePaymentSuccess(PaymentSuccessEvent  event)
{
        // Step 7: Complete the order processing

orderRepository.updateStatus(event.getOrderId()
, "COMPLETED");
    }


@KafkaListener(topics    =    "order-topic",
groupId = "order-group")
    public                          void
handleInventoryFailure(InventoryFailureEvent
event) {
        // Compensating action: Cancel the order

orderRepository.deleteById(event.getOrderId());
    }


@KafkaListener(topics    =    "order-topic",
groupId = "order-group")
    public                          void
handlePaymentFailure(PaymentFailureEvent  event)
{
```

```
        // Compensating action: Cancel the order
and  notify  Inventory  Service  to  release  the
product

orderRepository.deleteById(event.getOrderId());
        kafkaTemplate.send("inventory-topic",
new ReleaseProductEvent(event.getOrderId()));
    }

}
```

Step 3: SAGA Execution Flow

1. **Order Service** creates an order and emits an `OrderCreatedEvent` to the **Inventory Service**.

2. **Inventory Service** reserves the product and emits a `ProductReservedEvent` to the **Payment Service**.

3. **Payment Service** processes the payment and emits a `PaymentSuccessEvent` or `PaymentFailureEvent` based on the outcome.

4. If the payment is successful, the **Order Service** completes the order.

5. If any step fails, compensating actions are triggered to ensure consistency (e.g., canceling the order or releasing inventory).

Step 4: Managing Transactions and Compensation

In case of failure, the **compensating actions** ensure that the distributed transaction is rolled back to maintain data consistency. For example:

- If payment fails, the **inventory** is released.
- If the inventory reservation fails, the **order** is canceled.

By using the **SAGA pattern**, we can achieve **eventual consistency** without the need for complex distributed transactions or locking mechanisms.

Summary

In this chapter, we covered how to handle **distributed transactions** in a **microservices** architecture using the **SAGA pattern**. Key points included:

- **Challenges** **of** **distributed** **transactions** in microservices, including managing consistency and handling failures.
- **The SAGA pattern** as a solution for managing distributed transactions by breaking them down into local transactions with compensating actions.

- A real-world example of implementing the **SAGA pattern** in Java using **Spring Boot** and an **event-driven approach** with Kafka.

By applying the SAGA pattern, microservices can maintain consistency while handling failures in a distributed system, ensuring that the system remains reliable and resilient. In the next chapters, we will explore more advanced topics like **security**, **monitoring**, and **scalability** in microservices architectures.

CHAPTER 19

EVENT-DRIVEN MICROSERVICES

In this chapter, we will explore the concept of **event-driven microservices** and delve into advanced patterns like **Event Sourcing** and **CQRS (Command Query Responsibility Segregation)**. These patterns are key to building scalable, resilient, and efficient microservices that rely on events to drive communication and state changes. We will also go through a **real-world example** of implementing an event-driven architecture in Java, highlighting its benefits in a microservices environment.

The Concept of Event Sourcing and CQRS (Command Query Responsibility Segregation)

1. Event Sourcing: Event Sourcing is an architectural pattern where state transitions are stored as a sequence of **events** rather than maintaining the current state of an entity. Each event represents a change in the system, and the current state of the entity can be reconstructed by replaying the sequence of events that led to it.

In traditional systems, the state of an entity (e.g., an order) is stored in a **database table**, and changes to the state (e.g., updating the order status) are recorded directly in the database. However, in **Event Sourcing**, instead of storing just the current state, all state changes are captured as events (e.g., "OrderPlaced", "OrderShipped", "OrderDelivered").

Benefits of Event Sourcing:

- **Auditability**: All state changes are captured as events, providing an audit trail of how an entity arrived at its current state.
- **Rebuildability**: If the state of an entity needs to be reconstructed (e.g., after a failure), it can be done by replaying the events.
- **Decoupling**: Event sourcing allows services to communicate asynchronously via events, reducing tight coupling between services.

Example of Event Sourcing: Consider an **Order Service**. Instead of storing the current state of an order in a database, the service stores events such as:

- `OrderCreatedEvent`
- `OrderPaidEvent`
- `OrderShippedEvent`

To rebuild the current state of an order, we replay the events in the order they were created.

```java
public class Order {
    private Long id;
    private String status;

    public void apply(OrderCreatedEvent event) {
        this.id = event.getOrderId();
        this.status = "Created";
    }

    public void apply(OrderPaidEvent event) {
        this.status = "Paid";
    }

    public void apply(OrderShippedEvent event) {
        this.status = "Shipped";
    }
}
```

In this example, the `Order` class applies the events as they are received to update its state.

2. Command Query Responsibility Segregation (CQRS):
CQRS is another architectural pattern that separates the **command** side (which modifies data) and the **query** side (which retrieves

data) of the application. This allows the system to optimize both **reads** and **writes** independently.

In CQRS, the **write side** (command side) handles commands that change the state (e.g., placing an order, updating an order), while the **read side** (query side) handles queries that retrieve data (e.g., fetching order details). This separation allows for different data models and optimizations on both sides.

- **Commands** are used to modify the state of an entity, and they do not return data.
- **Queries** are used to retrieve data but do not modify the state.

Benefits of CQRS:

- **Optimized for reads and writes**: By separating the two, you can scale reads and writes independently, allowing each to be optimized for its use case.
- **Simplified data models**: Since the read and write models are separated, you can design them to fit their respective purposes (e.g., the read model could be denormalized for faster querying).
- **Better performance and scalability**: You can handle high read loads separately from write loads, which is especially useful in systems with high transaction volumes.

Real-World Example of Implementing Event-Driven Microservices in Java

Let's consider a **banking system** with two microservices: a **Transaction Service** and an **Account Service**. The **Transaction Service** handles financial transactions, while the **Account Service** manages user accounts and balances. The services need to communicate asynchronously and maintain consistent state.

1. **Step 1: Define Events:** We define several events that will represent state changes in the system, such as:

- `TransactionCreatedEvent`: Triggered when a new transaction is created.
- `TransactionCompletedEvent`: Triggered when a transaction is completed successfully.
- `AccountBalanceUpdatedEvent`: Triggered when the account balance is updated after a transaction.

2. **Step 2: Create Event Classes:**

```java
java

public class TransactionCreatedEvent {
    private Long transactionId;
    private Long accountId;
    private Double amount;
```

213

```
    // Constructors, getters, and setters
}

public class TransactionCompletedEvent {
    private Long transactionId;
    private String status;

    // Constructors, getters, and setters
}

public class AccountBalanceUpdatedEvent {
    private Long accountId;
    private Double newBalance;

    // Constructors, getters, and setters
}
```

3. Step 3: Implement Event-Driven Communication with Kafka:

In an event-driven system, services communicate via **events**. We can use **Kafka** as the event broker to transmit these events between the **Transaction Service** and the **Account Service**.

Transaction Service (Producer):

```java
java
```

```java
@Service
public class TransactionService {

    @Autowired
    private                 KafkaTemplate<String,
TransactionCreatedEvent> kafkaTemplate;

    public  void  createTransaction(Transaction
transaction) {
        // Create transaction in the database

transactionRepository.save(transaction);

        // Emit the TransactionCreatedEvent to
Kafka
        kafkaTemplate.send("transaction-topic",
new TransactionCreatedEvent(transaction.getId(),
transaction.getAccountId(),
transaction.getAmount())));
    }
}
```

Account Service (Consumer):

java

```java
@Service
public class AccountService {
```

```java
@KafkaListener(topics = "transaction-topic",
groupId = "account-service")
public                              void
handleTransactionCreated(TransactionCreatedEven
t event) {
        // Fetch account details and update
balance
        Account        account        =
accountRepository.findById(event.getAccountId()
);

        Double newBalance = account.getBalance()
- event.getAmount();
        account.setBalance(newBalance);
        accountRepository.save(account);

        // Emit AccountBalanceUpdatedEvent to
Kafka
        kafkaTemplate.send("account-topic",  new
AccountBalanceUpdatedEvent(event.getAccountId()
, newBalance));
    }
}
```

In this example, the **Transaction Service** publishes the
TransactionCreatedEvent when a transaction is created. The
Account Service listens for this event, updates the account
balance, and then emits an AccountBalanceUpdatedEvent to
notify other services or systems about the updated balance.

4. Step 4: Event Sourcing and CQRS in Action:

If we want to incorporate **Event Sourcing**, instead of saving the current state of the transaction or account in a database, we would save the events (e.g., `TransactionCreatedEvent`, `AccountBalanceUpdatedEvent`) and reconstruct the state from these events.

For **CQRS**, we would separate the read and write models. The **write model** would handle commands like creating a transaction or updating an account balance, while the **read model** would be optimized for querying account balances or transaction history.

Example of Read and Write Model Separation:

- **Write Model (Command)**: Contains logic to execute a command (e.g., creating a transaction, updating the account balance).
- **Read Model (Query)**: Contains optimized views or projections for querying data (e.g., account balance, transaction history).

5. Step 5: Using an Event Store for Event Sourcing:

To fully implement **Event Sourcing**, you can use an event store to persist the events and replay them to rebuild the state. There are specialized event stores like **EventStoreDB** or you could use a database like **Cassandra** or **Kafka** itself as the event store.

Example event store:

java

```java
public class EventStore {

    private final List<Event> events = new
ArrayList<>();

    public void saveEvent(Event event) {
        events.add(event);
    }

    public List<Event> getEvents() {
        return events;
    }
}
```

This `EventStore` stores events, which can later be used to rebuild the state of an entity (e.g., an account) by replaying the events.

Benefits of Event-Driven Architecture

1. Scalability: Event-driven systems can scale better than synchronous, request-response architectures. By using events, you decouple services and allow them to scale independently. For example, if there are many transactions, the **Transaction Service**

can scale independently of the **Account Service** by handling events asynchronously.

2. Resilience and Fault Tolerance: If a service fails or is temporarily unavailable, events can be queued and processed later, providing **resilience**. Additionally, services can implement **compensating actions** (e.g., rolling back a transaction) to handle failures.

3. Flexibility: Event-driven architectures allow for more flexible and decoupled communication between services. Adding new services to the system becomes easier as they can subscribe to existing events without impacting the other services.

4. Real-time Processing: Event-driven systems excel at real-time data processing. For example, an e-commerce system could react to an order event in real-time by updating inventory or triggering a shipment notification.

5. Improved Maintainability: Event-driven architectures can be easier to maintain because services are more isolated. This reduces the complexity of updating one service without affecting others. Since each service only listens to and reacts to the relevant events, changes can be made independently.

Summary

In this chapter, we covered **Event-Driven Microservices**, including key patterns like **Event Sourcing** and **CQRS**. We explored:

- **Event Sourcing**: Storing state changes as events and reconstructing the state by replaying those events.
- **CQRS**: Separating the command and query models to optimize both for their respective use cases.
- **Event-driven architecture**: A model that uses events to drive communication and state changes between microservices.

We implemented a **real-world example** using **Kafka** to demonstrate how microservices can communicate via events and how to manage distributed transactions. We also highlighted the **benefits** of event-driven architectures, including **scalability**, **resilience**, **flexibility**, and **real-time processing**.

In the next chapters, we will explore **advanced patterns** like **saga** for managing distributed transactions and **distributed tracing** for improving observability in microservices.

CHAPTER 20

API GATEWAY AND GATEWAY OFFLOADING

In this chapter, we will explore the concept of the **API Gateway** pattern, which is a key architectural pattern for managing and securing microservices. We will discuss how to set up a **Spring Cloud Gateway** for your microservices, and how to offload responsibilities such as **authentication**, **routing**, and **rate-limiting** to the API Gateway. By centralizing these tasks in the API Gateway, you can simplify the management of microservices and improve the overall security and performance of the system.

Introduction to API Gateway Pattern

An **API Gateway** is a server that acts as an entry point for client requests to a microservices system. It routes requests to the appropriate backend service, aggregates responses, and can perform additional tasks such as **authentication**, **logging**, **rate limiting**, and **caching**.

In a microservices architecture, the **API Gateway pattern** serves as a **reverse proxy** for all incoming requests, forwarding them to the relevant microservices. It can also provide a unified API to

221

clients, making the system easier to interact with, even if there are multiple backend services.

Key Benefits of API Gateway Pattern:

1. **Simplified Client Interaction**: The API Gateway provides a single point of entry for clients, reducing the complexity of making requests to multiple microservices.

2. **Centralized Management**: By centralizing tasks like routing, authentication, and rate-limiting, you can reduce the workload on individual microservices and make the system easier to manage.

3. **Security**: The API Gateway can handle **authentication** and **authorization**, ensuring that only authorized users can access the microservices.

4. **Traffic Management**: The API Gateway can perform **rate-limiting**, **request throttling**, and **load balancing**, helping to optimize the system's performance and resilience.

Setting Up a Spring Cloud Gateway for Microservices

Spring Cloud Gateway is a popular choice for implementing an API Gateway in a **Spring Boot** microservices architecture. It provides a simple and effective way to route requests, manage

APIs, and offload cross-cutting concerns such as authentication, logging, and rate-limiting.

1. Adding Spring Cloud Gateway Dependencies: To get started with **Spring Cloud Gateway**, you need to add the necessary dependencies to your `pom.xml` or `build.gradle` file.

Maven Configuration:

```xml
xml

<dependency>

<groupId>org.springframework.cloud</groupId>
    <artifactId>spring-cloud-starter-
gateway</artifactId>
</dependency>
<dependency>

<groupId>org.springframework.cloud</groupId>
    <artifactId>spring-cloud-starter-netflix-
eureka-client</artifactId>
</dependency>
```

Gradle Configuration:

```gradle
gradle

dependencies {
```

223

```
    implementation
'org.springframework.cloud:spring-cloud-
starter-gateway'
    implementation
'org.springframework.cloud:spring-cloud-
starter-netflix-eureka-client'
}
```

2. Configuring Spring Cloud Gateway: Once the dependencies are added, you can configure the **Spring Cloud Gateway** to route incoming requests to the appropriate microservices. The gateway can be configured using **application.properties** or **application.yml**.

Example configuration (application.yml):

yaml

```
spring:
  cloud:
    gateway:
      routes:
        - id: product-service
          uri: lb://PRODUCT-SERVICE
          predicates:
            - Path=/products/**
        - id: order-service
          uri: lb://ORDER-SERVICE
          predicates:
```

```
- Path=/orders/**
```

Explanation:

- `uri: lb://PRODUCT-SERVICE`: This URI indicates that the request will be routed to the `PRODUCT-SERVICE`, which is registered in **Eureka** for service discovery.
- `predicates`: These define the conditions under which a route should be triggered. In this case, requests to `/products/**` will be routed to the `PRODUCT-SERVICE`, and requests to `/orders/**` will be routed to the `ORDER-SERVICE`.

3. Running the Spring Cloud Gateway: Once the configuration is complete, you can run the Spring Cloud Gateway application just like any other Spring Boot application. It will automatically start listening for incoming requests on port 8080 (by default) and route them to the appropriate backend services based on the defined routes.

Offloading Authentication, Routing, and Rate-Limiting to the API Gateway

One of the major benefits of using an API Gateway is the ability to offload common tasks such as **authentication, routing,** and

rate-limiting from individual microservices, centralizing these concerns in the gateway.

1. Offloading Authentication to the API Gateway: Instead of implementing authentication logic in each microservice, the API Gateway can handle authentication and forward only authenticated requests to the backend services. You can integrate the API Gateway with **OAuth2, JWT**, or any other authentication mechanism.

Example of adding **JWT authentication** to Spring Cloud Gateway:

```yaml
spring:
  cloud:
    gateway:
      routes:
        - id: product-service
          uri: lb://PRODUCT-SERVICE
          predicates:
            - Path=/products/**
          filters:
            - name: JwtAuthenticationFilter
        - id: order-service
          uri: lb://ORDER-SERVICE
          predicates:
            - Path=/orders/**
```

226

```
filters:
    - name: JwtAuthenticationFilter
```

In this example, the **JwtAuthenticationFilter** is responsible for validating the JWT token before routing the request to the product or order service.

You can also use **Spring Security** to configure authentication in the API Gateway:

java

```
@EnableWebSecurity
public class GatewaySecurityConfig extends
WebSecurityConfigurerAdapter {

    @Override
    protected void configure(HttpSecurity http)
throws Exception {
        http
            .authorizeRequests()
            .antMatchers("/products/**",
"/orders/**").authenticated()
            .and()
            .oauth2Login(); // Configure OAuth2
login if needed
    }
}
```

227

2. Offloading Routing to the API Gateway: Routing is the main responsibility of the API Gateway. It routes incoming requests to the appropriate microservices based on the defined rules and conditions.

For more complex routing, you can use filters to modify the request or add custom logic.

Example of a custom filter to add a header:

java

```
@Bean
public GlobalFilter customFilter() {
    return (exchange, chain) -> {

exchange.getRequest().mutate().header("X-
Custom-Header", "MyHeaderValue");
        return chain.filter(exchange);
    };
}
```

This filter adds a custom header (X-Custom-Header) to every request before it reaches the backend service.

3. Offloading Rate-Limiting to the API Gateway: Rate-limiting ensures that your microservices are not overwhelmed by too many requests. The API Gateway can handle **rate-limiting** for all

228

incoming requests and protect the backend services from excessive load.

Spring Cloud Gateway allows you to configure **rate-limiting** filters using **Redis** as the backend for storing rate limits.

Example configuration for rate-limiting in `application.yml`:

```yaml
spring:
  cloud:
    gateway:
      routes:
        - id: product-service
          uri: lb://PRODUCT-SERVICE
          predicates:
            - Path=/products/**
          filters:
            - name: RequestRateLimiter
              args:
                redis-rate-limiter.replenishRate: 10
                redis-rate-limiter.burstCapacity: 20
```

In this configuration:

- `replenishRate`: Specifies how many requests per second are allowed.

- `burstCapacity`: Specifies how many requests can be handled in a burst before the rate limiter starts rejecting requests.

Real-World Example: Setting Up Logging and Monitoring for the API Gateway

In a production environment, it's crucial to monitor the health, performance, and traffic of the API Gateway to ensure the system's reliability. Logging and monitoring are essential for identifying issues early and maintaining the health of your microservices ecosystem.

1. Logging Requests: You can log the incoming requests to the API Gateway for audit and debugging purposes. This can be done by implementing a filter that logs each request:

java

```
@Bean
public GlobalFilter loggingFilter() {
    return (exchange, chain) -> {
        log.info("Request:          "          +
exchange.getRequest().getURI());
        return chain.filter(exchange);
```

```
    };
}
```

This filter logs the URI of every request before it is routed to the corresponding service.

2. Monitoring the API Gateway: Use **Spring Boot Actuator** to expose health and metrics endpoints for monitoring the API Gateway. You can integrate with **Prometheus** and **Grafana** to visualize metrics and set up alerts.

For example, you can expose a custom health check in the application.yml:

yaml

```
management:
  endpoints:
    web:
      exposure:
        include: health, metrics
```

You can then scrape these metrics in **Prometheus** and visualize them in **Grafana**.

Summary

In this chapter, we explored the **API Gateway** pattern, focusing on how it simplifies and centralizes tasks like **authentication, routing**, and **rate-limiting** in a microservices architecture. The key takeaways include:

- **API Gateway** provides a unified entry point for clients and handles cross-cutting concerns such as authentication, routing, and rate-limiting.
- We set up a **Spring Cloud Gateway** to route requests to different microservices based on conditions like path matching.
- Authentication, routing, and rate-limiting were offloaded to the API Gateway, reducing the complexity of individual microservices.
- We discussed the importance of **logging** and **monitoring** the API Gateway for better system observability.

The API Gateway plays a crucial role in optimizing microservices communication, improving security, and simplifying the overall architecture. In the next chapters, we will explore further topics like **service mesh architectures, scaling microservices**, and **best practices for security**.

CHAPTER 21

SECURITY BEST PRACTICES FOR MICROSERVICES

In this chapter, we will explore **security best practices** for building secure and resilient **microservices**. Microservices architectures introduce unique security challenges because services are distributed and often communicate over the network. These challenges make securing microservices critical to protect sensitive data, prevent unauthorized access, and ensure the overall integrity of the system.

We will discuss **common security vulnerabilities**, how to implement **HTTPS, SSL/TLS** for securing communication between microservices, and **best practices** for securing data in transit and at rest.

Common Security Vulnerabilities in Microservices

Microservices architectures, by their nature, can introduce several vulnerabilities that need to be addressed to ensure the security of the system. Some of the most common security risks in microservices include:

233

1. Unauthorized Access and Authentication Issues: Microservices typically communicate over HTTP, which makes it important to ensure that only authorized users or services can access sensitive endpoints. Without proper **authentication** and **authorization**, malicious users could exploit the system to access or modify resources.

- **Solution:** Use a strong **authentication** mechanism, such as **OAuth2** or **JWT** (JSON Web Tokens), for ensuring that only authenticated clients can make requests to the services.

2. Lack of Proper Authorization: While a service might be authenticated, it is still crucial to ensure that it has the right **permissions** to access specific resources. Without **role-based access control (RBAC)** or **attribute-based access control (ABAC)**, an authenticated service might have access to resources it should not.

- **Solution:** Implement fine-grained **authorization** mechanisms to control access to specific resources based on the roles or attributes of the user/service.

3. Data Exposure and Insecure Data Communication: Data transmitted over the network could be intercepted if not properly secured. Without encryption, sensitive data like **user credentials,**

234

personal information, and **financial data** can be exposed to attackers.

- **Solution:** Use **HTTPS**, which ensures that data in transit is encrypted using **SSL/TLS**, to protect sensitive data from being intercepted.

4. Insecure APIs and Endpoints: Microservices expose APIs that can be targeted by attackers. Poorly designed APIs or APIs that are not properly validated can lead to vulnerabilities such as **SQL injection**, **cross-site scripting (XSS)**, and **denial of service (DoS)** attacks.

- **Solution:** Validate all inputs, sanitize user data, and use security best practices for API development to avoid common attack vectors.

5. Service-to-Service Communication: Microservices often communicate with each other over the network, which can create vulnerabilities if these communications are not properly secured. For example, if an attacker gains access to one microservice, they could potentially exploit service-to-service communication to gain access to other services.

- **Solution:** Use **mutual TLS (mTLS)** for securing internal service-to-service communication and implement **service mesh** technologies like **Istio** to manage security and enforce policies between services.

235

Implementing HTTPS, SSL/TLS in Microservices

1. Understanding SSL/TLS for Microservices Security: SSL (Secure Sockets Layer) and **TLS (Transport Layer Security)** are cryptographic protocols used to ensure secure communication between clients and servers. While SSL is now considered outdated and deprecated, **TLS** is the industry standard for encrypting communications.

When implementing **HTTPS** for microservices, **SSL/TLS** is used to:

- **Encrypt data in transit**: Prevent unauthorized parties from eavesdropping on sensitive data being transmitted between clients and microservices.
- **Authenticate services**: Ensure that the communication is occurring with the intended service, preventing man-in-the-middle (MITM) attacks.

2. Setting Up HTTPS with SSL/TLS for Java Microservices: To secure your microservices, you need to configure them to use **HTTPS** by generating and using **SSL certificates**. Here's how you can set up **SSL/TLS** in **Spring Boot** microservices:

- **Generate an SSL Certificate**: You can generate a self-signed SSL certificate using the keytool utility provided by Java. Here's an example of how to generate a keystore with a self-signed certificate:

```bash
```

```
keytool -genkey -keyalg RSA -keysize 2048
-alias mysslkey -keystore keystore.jks -
validity 365
```

This generates a keystore file (`keystore.jks`) containing the SSL certificate.

- **Configure Spring Boot for SSL:** Once you have the keystore, you can configure Spring Boot to use **HTTPS** by specifying the keystore location and password in the `application.properties` or `application.yml` file:

```properties
```

```
server.ssl.key-
store=classpath:keystore.jks
server.ssl.key-store-password=my-password
server.ssl.key-store-type=JKS
server.ssl.key-alias=mysslkey
server.port=8443  # Default HTTPS port
```

This configuration enables HTTPS on the Spring Boot application and configures it to use the generated keystore.

3. Implementing Mutual TLS (mTLS): For **service-to-service communication**, you can implement **mutual TLS (mTLS)** to ensure that both parties (the client and server) authenticate each other. In mTLS, both the client and the server must present valid certificates before communication is allowed.

To implement mTLS in a Spring Boot microservice, you can configure both the client and server to use their certificates for mutual authentication. Here's an example of the server-side configuration:

```properties
server.ssl.key-store=classpath:server-keystore.jks
server.ssl.key-store-password=server-password
server.ssl.key-store-type=JKS
server.ssl.key-alias=server-key
server.ssl.client-auth=need
```

The `client-auth=need` setting ensures that the server requires the client to present a certificate for authentication.

238

Best Practices: Securing Data in Transit and at Rest

1. Securing Data in Transit: Data in transit refers to data that is being transferred over a network. Since microservices often communicate over HTTP or other protocols, it is essential to ensure that this data is encrypted to prevent **eavesdropping** or **man-in-the-middle (MITM)** attacks.

- **Use HTTPS (SSL/TLS)**: As discussed earlier, ensure that all communication between clients and microservices is done over HTTPS to protect sensitive data from being intercepted during transmission.

- **Mutual TLS (mTLS) for Service Communication**: Use **mTLS** to ensure that microservices authenticate each other during communication, adding an additional layer of security for inter-service communication.

2. Securing Data at Rest: Data at rest refers to data that is stored on disk, such as in databases, file systems, or object storage. It's equally important to protect this data to prevent unauthorized access.

- **Database Encryption**: Enable **transparent data encryption (TDE)** in your database to encrypt sensitive data stored in database tables. Most database systems, including **MySQL**, **PostgreSQL**, and **MongoDB**, offer built-in encryption mechanisms for data at rest.

- **File Encryption**: If your microservices store sensitive data in files (e.g., logs, images), make sure to encrypt those files before storing them. You can use libraries like **JCE (Java Cryptography Extension)** to encrypt files in Java.

- **Key Management**: Use a centralized key management system (KMS) to store and manage encryption keys securely. **AWS KMS, HashiCorp Vault**, or **Azure Key Vault** are good examples of secure key management solutions.

3. Security Headers: Ensure that your microservices respond with proper **security headers** to defend against attacks such as **cross-site scripting (XSS), clickjacking**, and **content sniffing**.

Example Spring Security configuration to add security headers:

```java
http
    .headers()
        .contentSecurityPolicy("default-src
'self'")
        .and()
    .frameOptions().deny()
    .and()
```

```
.httpStrictTransportSecurity().maxAgeInSeconds(
31536000).includeSubDomains(true)
    .and()
    .xssProtection().block(true);
```

These headers ensure that the application is more resilient against certain types of attacks.

Summary

In this chapter, we covered the essential security practices for securing **microservices**:

- We discussed the **common security vulnerabilities** in microservices, including issues related to authentication, authorization, and data exposure.
- We explored how to implement **HTTPS** and **SSL/TLS** for securing data in transit between microservices, including **mutual TLS (mTLS)** for service-to-service authentication.
- We highlighted best practices for **securing data at rest**, including **database encryption** and **file encryption**, as well as the use of **key management systems**.
- We also discussed how to add **security headers** to protect against attacks such as **XSS** and **clickjacking**.

By implementing these security practices, you can ensure that your microservices are resilient, secure, and capable of protecting sensitive data. In the next chapters, we will continue to explore best practices for **scaling, monitoring,** and **maintaining the security** of your microservices in a production environment.

CHAPTER 22

MICROSERVICES WITH SERVERLESS ARCHITECTURES

In this chapter, we will explore **serverless architectures** and how they can be used to build scalable, cost-efficient **microservices**. Serverless computing has gained significant popularity due to its ability to reduce infrastructure management overhead and allow developers to focus more on application logic rather than on the infrastructure. We will cover the basics of serverless computing, how services like **AWS Lambda** and **Azure Functions** can be used for microservices, and provide a **real-world example** of integrating **serverless functions** with **Java-based microservices**.

Introduction to Serverless Computing

What is Serverless Computing? Serverless computing is an execution model where cloud providers automatically manage the infrastructure required to run application code. In this model, the developer writes functions or code without worrying about the underlying servers, scaling, or managing resources. Instead, these functions run in stateless, ephemeral containers that are provisioned and scaled automatically by the cloud provider.

243

While the term "serverless" implies the absence of servers, it actually refers to the abstraction of server management. Servers are still involved, but developers do not need to manage them directly.

Key Features of Serverless Computing:

1. **Event-driven**: Serverless functions are typically invoked by events, such as HTTP requests, file uploads, or messages in a queue.

2. **Automatic Scaling**: Serverless platforms automatically scale the execution of functions in response to incoming demand. For example, if the number of requests increases, the platform can spin up new instances to handle the load.

3. **Pay-per-Use**: With serverless computing, you only pay for the compute resources that your functions consume while they are running. There is no need to provision or manage servers, so costs are based on usage.

4. **Short-lived Execution**: Serverless functions typically execute in short bursts, such as processing an HTTP request or performing a background task. The platform provisions resources only when the function is called and automatically terminates them when the function completes.

Using AWS Lambda or Azure Functions for Microservices

1. AWS Lambda: AWS Lambda is a serverless compute service provided by Amazon Web Services (AWS). It allows you to run code without provisioning or managing servers. Lambda functions can be triggered by various AWS services such as **API Gateway**, **S3**, **DynamoDB**, and **SNS**, among others.

Benefits of Using AWS Lambda for Microservices:

- **Automatic Scaling**: Lambda scales automatically to handle large volumes of incoming requests without any manual intervention.
- **Integrated with AWS Ecosystem**: Lambda integrates well with other AWS services, making it easy to build microservices that communicate with databases, storage, and messaging systems.
- **Cost-Effective**: With Lambda, you only pay for the execution time of your functions, which makes it an economical option for microservices.

Creating a Simple AWS Lambda Function: To create a Lambda function that handles HTTP requests (using **API Gateway**), follow these steps:

1. Write a simple function in Java:

```java
```

```
public    class    ProductHandler    implements
RequestHandler<Map<String,           String>,
String> {
    @Override
    public                              String
handleRequest(Map<String,  String>  input,
Context context) {
        String        productId        =
input.get("productId");
        // Simulate  retrieving  product
details
        return   "Product   details   for
product ID: " + productId;
    }
}
```

2. Deploy the Lambda function via the AWS Management Console or AWS CLI.

3. Set up **API Gateway** to trigger the Lambda function whenever an HTTP request is received:

   o Create an API Gateway resource and method (e.g., GET `/product/{id}`).

   o Set the method to trigger the Lambda function.

2. Azure Functions: Azure Functions is Microsoft's serverless compute service, part of the **Azure** cloud platform. Like AWS Lambda, it enables you to run code in response to various events, such as HTTP requests, messages in a queue, or database updates.

Benefits of Using Azure Functions for Microservices:

- **Integration with Azure Ecosystem**: Azure Functions integrates seamlessly with other Azure services such as **Azure Blob Storage**, **Azure Cosmos DB**, and **Azure Service Bus**, allowing you to create a complete microservices architecture.
- **Scaling and Cost**: Similar to AWS Lambda, Azure Functions automatically scale and are billed based on execution time, making them a cost-effective choice for microservices.

Creating a Simple Azure Function: In Azure Functions, you can write a function using Java, similar to how you would use AWS Lambda. Here's an example of a simple HTTP-triggered function:

1. Define the function:

```java
@FunctionName("ProductFunction")
public String run(
    @HttpTrigger(name = "req", methods = {HttpMethod.GET}, authLevel = AuthorizationLevel.FUNCTION)
HttpRequestMessage<Optional<String>> request,
    final ExecutionContext context
) {
```

247

```
  String           productId          =
request.getQueryParameters().get("product
Id");
      return "Product details for product ID:
" + productId;
  }
```

2. Deploy the function using **Azure CLI** or through the Azure portal.

3. Use **Azure API Management** or **Azure Functions Proxies** to expose the function as an API.

Real-World Example: Integrating Serverless Functions with Java-Based Microservices

Let's look at an example of integrating **serverless functions** with **Java-based microservices**. In this scenario, we are building an e-commerce system with the following microservices:

- **Product Service**: Manages product details.
- **Order Service**: Handles customer orders.

We want to integrate **AWS Lambda** for processing orders asynchronously whenever a customer places an order, and use **API Gateway** to expose the Lambda function.

Step 1: Product Service (Java-based Microservice)

The **Product Service** is a traditional Java-based microservice that provides product information to customers. It exposes a REST API to fetch product details.

Example using **Spring Boot**:

```java
@RestController
@RequestMapping("/products")
public class ProductController {

    @Autowired
    private ProductService productService;

    @GetMapping("/{id}")
    public              ResponseEntity<Product>
getProduct(@PathVariable Long id) {
        Product          product          =
productService.getProductById(id);
        return ResponseEntity.ok(product);
    }
}
```

Step 2: Order Service (Serverless Function)

The **Order Service** needs to process customer orders asynchronously. Instead of handling order processing inside the service, we can offload this to an **AWS Lambda function**.

Order Processing Lambda:

```java
public class OrderProcessingHandler implements
RequestHandler<Map<String, String>, String> {
    @Override
    public String handleRequest(Map<String,
String> input, Context context) {
        String orderId = input.get("orderId");
        // Simulate order processing logic
        return "Order " + orderId + " processed
successfully!";
    }
}
```

Step 3: Integrating Order Service with AWS Lambda

When a customer places an order in the **Order Service**, we send an event to **AWS Lambda** for processing the order. This event can be triggered by calling the Lambda function directly via **AWS SDK** or using **API Gateway** to trigger the function via HTTP requests.

Order Service Example:

```java
@Service
```

```
public class OrderService {

    private final AWSLambda awsLambda;

    @Autowired
    public OrderService(AWSLambda awsLambda) {
        this.awsLambda = awsLambda;
    }

    public void placeOrder(Order order) {
        // Save order to database
        orderRepository.save(order);

        // Trigger Lambda function for order
processing
        InvokeRequest    invokeRequest    =    new
InvokeRequest()

.withFunctionName("orderProcessingFunction")
            .withPayload("{\"orderId\":\""     +
order.getId() + "\"}");

        awsLambda.invoke(invokeRequest);
    }
}
```

In this example:

- The **Order Service** saves the order and sends the order details to the **AWS Lambda function** for further

251

processing (e.g., updating inventory, sending confirmation email).

- The **Lambda function** processes the order asynchronously, freeing up the microservice to handle other requests without delay.

Step 4: Connecting AWS Lambda with API Gateway

We can also expose the Lambda function via **API Gateway** to allow external clients or other services to trigger the order processing flow.

1. Create an API in **API Gateway** that triggers the **AWS Lambda function** when a request is received.
2. Secure the API with **API keys** or **OAuth2** to ensure only authorized users or services can trigger the function.

Benefits of Event-Driven Serverless Architecture

1. Cost Efficiency: Serverless functions only consume resources when they are invoked, and you only pay for the execution time. This is cost-effective, especially for microservices that have unpredictable or low traffic patterns.

2. Scalability: Serverless functions automatically scale based on demand. If more orders come in, AWS Lambda or Azure

Functions can scale up to handle them without manual intervention.

3. Simplified Infrastructure Management: With serverless architectures, you don't have to manage the underlying infrastructure. The cloud provider automatically handles scaling, provisioning, and maintenance of resources.

4. Flexibility and Decoupling: Serverless functions allow services to be **loosely coupled**. In our example, the **Order Service** does not need to know the specifics of order processing; it simply triggers a Lambda function, which handles the logic independently.

5. Event-Driven Communication: Serverless functions work well in event-driven architectures, allowing different services to react to events asynchronously. This makes the system more resilient and responsive.

Summary

In this chapter, we discussed **serverless computing** and its application in **microservices architectures**. Key points include:

- **Serverless computing** abstracts away infrastructure management, allowing developers to focus on code rather than scaling and provisioning resources.

- We explored how to use **AWS Lambda** and **Azure Functions** for building microservices in a serverless environment, including an example of integrating serverless functions with a Java-based **Order Service**.

- We discussed the **benefits of serverless architectures**, such as **cost efficiency**, **scalability**, and **flexibility**, which make them ideal for certain use cases in microservices.

In the following chapters, we will continue to explore best practices for scaling, securing, and monitoring microservices, with a focus on **serverless architecture** as an evolving and powerful tool for modern application development.

CHAPTER 23

OPTIMIZING MICROSERVICES PERFORMANCE

In this chapter, we will focus on **optimizing the performance** of microservices to ensure that they can handle high traffic loads, respond quickly to user requests, and scale efficiently. Microservices, by their nature, can suffer from performance bottlenecks due to distributed architectures, slow network communication, or inefficient data storage. We will explore how to **identify** these bottlenecks, apply **caching strategies** using tools like **Redis**, and provide a **real-world example** of performance tuning for high-traffic microservices.

Identifying and Solving Performance Bottlenecks

1. Common Performance Bottlenecks in Microservices: In microservices architectures, there are several common causes of performance bottlenecks. Identifying these issues early is critical to maintaining a responsive and scalable system.

- **Slow Database Queries**: As microservices often use their own databases, inefficient database queries can slow down response times. This could be due to poorly

255

designed queries, missing indexes, or high contention in database connections.

- **Network Latency**: Microservices typically communicate over the network (e.g., HTTP or gRPC). High network latency can significantly affect performance, especially when services are deployed in different regions or on different networks.

- **Overloaded Services**: If a particular microservice becomes a bottleneck, all dependent services may suffer. For instance, a single service handling too many requests or performing resource-heavy operations could degrade the performance of the entire system.

- **Synchronous Communication**: Microservices often communicate synchronously, meaning that a request must wait for a response from another service before it can proceed. This can lead to **request chaining** or **service dependency delays**, resulting in slower response times.

- **Resource Exhaustion**: Running out of resources, such as CPU, memory, or network bandwidth, can also cause performance degradation. It's essential to monitor and adjust resource allocations to avoid this issue.

2. Tools for Identifying Performance Bottlenecks:

- **Profiling**: Use profiling tools (e.g., **JProfiler**, **VisualVM**) to track CPU and memory usage and identify which parts of the code are consuming excessive resources.

- **Distributed Tracing**: Tools like **Jaeger** and **Zipkin** allow you to trace requests as they pass through different microservices. This helps in identifying the specific service or operation that is slowing down the overall system.

- **Metrics and Monitoring**: Use tools like **Prometheus** and **Grafana** to collect and visualize performance metrics, such as CPU and memory usage, request throughput, and response times.

Caching Strategies: Redis, In-Memory Caching

1. Why Caching is Important in Microservices: Caching is a key strategy for improving the performance of microservices, especially for frequently accessed data or computationally expensive operations. By storing data in a **cache**, you can avoid redundant database queries or API calls, thus reducing response times and improving overall system performance.

2. Types of Caching:

- **In-Memory Caching**: Stores data in the memory of the application itself. It is extremely fast but limited by the available memory. Common tools for in-memory caching include **EhCache** and **Guava**.

- **Distributed Caching**: Stores data in a separate cache layer that can be accessed by multiple microservices. **Redis** is one of the most popular distributed caching solutions and allows data to be shared across different instances and services, making it ideal for high-traffic applications.

3. Using Redis for Caching:

Redis is an in-memory, key-value store that is widely used for caching in microservices. It can store various types of data, such as strings, lists, sets, and hashes, and provides fast read and write operations.

Setting Up Redis with Spring Boot:

To use Redis in a Spring Boot application, you can add the following dependency in your `pom.xml`:

xml

```
<dependency>
    <groupId>org.springframework.boot</groupId>
    <artifactId>spring-boot-starter-data-
redis</artifactId>
</dependency>
```

Then, configure Redis in your **application.properties**:

```
properties
```

```
spring.redis.host=localhost
spring.redis.port=6379
spring.redis.password=password
```

Example of Caching with Redis:

Let's say we have a **ProductService** that fetches product details from a database. Instead of fetching the product data from the database every time, we can cache the result in Redis.

```java
@Service
public class ProductService {

    @Autowired
    private ProductRepository productRepository;

    @Autowired
    private RedisTemplate<String, Product>
redisTemplate;

    public Product getProductById(Long id) {
        String cacheKey = "product:" + id;
        Product cachedProduct =
redisTemplate.opsForValue().get(cacheKey);
```

```
if (cachedProduct != null) {
    return cachedProduct;
}

// If product not found in cache, fetch
from database
Product                product              =
productRepository.findById(id)
            .orElseThrow(()       ->      new
ProductNotFoundException("Product not found"));

// Cache the product data

redisTemplate.opsForValue().set(cacheKey,
product, 10, TimeUnit.MINUTES);

    return product;
  }
}
```

Explanation:

- **RedisTemplate**: A Spring Data Redis template for interacting with Redis.
- **opsForValue()**: Used to perform operations on simple key-value pairs (strings).
- **cacheKey**: The Redis key used to store the product data.

260

- **Expiration**: The cached product data is stored for 10 minutes before it expires.

4. Cache Invalidation: Cache invalidation is crucial to ensure that the cache reflects the latest data. Common strategies for cache invalidation include:

- **Time-based expiration**: Set an expiration time for cache entries.
- **Event-driven invalidation**: Invalidate or update the cache when certain events occur (e.g., when data is updated in the database).
- **Manual invalidation**: Programmatically clear or update the cache when needed.

Real-World Example: Performance Tuning for High-Traffic Microservices

Let's consider a **high-traffic e-commerce platform** with multiple microservices, including **Product Service**, **Order Service**, and **Payment Service**. These services need to handle thousands of requests per minute, so performance optimization is critical.

1. Problem: Slow Product Lookups The **Product Service** is responsible for fetching product details. With thousands of requests hitting the service, product lookups become a performance bottleneck. The database is slow to respond under heavy load, and the service struggles to keep up with the traffic.

Solution: Caching Product Data To solve this, we can cache frequently accessed product data using **Redis**. When a request is made to the **Product Service**, the service first checks the Redis cache for the product data. If the data is not found, it retrieves the data from the database and stores it in the cache for future use.

By using **Redis** for caching, we reduce the load on the database and decrease response times, especially for popular products that are frequently queried.

2. Problem: Slow Database Queries in Order Service The **Order Service** performs heavy database operations to track orders. As the traffic increases, the database queries become slower, leading to increased response times.

Solution: Database Query Optimization To address this, we can:

- **Optimize database queries** by adding indexes to frequently queried columns (e.g., `orderId`, `customerId`).
- **Use database connection pooling** to manage database connections efficiently and avoid connection contention.
- **Use batch processing** for writing or updating multiple orders at once to reduce database load.

3. Problem: Too Many Concurrent Requests Overloading Services When the system receives a sudden spike in traffic (e.g., during a flash sale), multiple microservices, including **Product Service**, **Order Service**, and **Payment Service**, become overloaded and slow down.

Solution: Rate Limiting and Load Balancing To mitigate this, we can implement **rate limiting** and **load balancing**:

- **Rate limiting**: Using Spring Cloud Gateway or an API Gateway, we can restrict the number of requests allowed from a single client within a specific time window (e.g., 100 requests per minute).
- **Load balancing**: We can horizontally scale services by adding more instances of the **Product Service** and **Order Service** to handle the increased traffic.

4. Problem: Slow Response Times for Payment Processing The **Payment Service** is responsible for processing payments via external payment gateways. These external calls can be slow and unpredictable, affecting the overall performance of the system.

Solution: Asynchronous Processing To solve this, we can offload payment processing to a background task and return an immediate response to the user, notifying them that the payment is being processed. This can be achieved by using:

- **Message queues** (e.g., **RabbitMQ**, **Kafka**) to asynchronously process payment requests.
- **Retry mechanisms** to handle transient failures from the external payment gateway.

Summary

In this chapter, we covered essential strategies for **optimizing the performance** of microservices, focusing on:

- **Identifying performance bottlenecks**, including slow database queries, network latency, overloaded services, and inefficient communication.
- **Caching strategies**, such as using **Redis** for caching frequently accessed data and improving response times by reducing the load on databases.
- **Real-world examples** of performance tuning for a high-traffic microservices environment, including caching product data, optimizing database queries, and implementing asynchronous processing for payment services.

By applying these optimization techniques, you can improve the responsiveness, scalability, and efficiency of your microservices architecture. In the next chapters, we will continue exploring best practices for **scaling** and **securing** microservices at scale.

CHAPTER 24

SCALING MICROSERVICES

In this chapter, we will focus on **scaling microservices** effectively, an essential aspect of ensuring that your microservices architecture can handle growing traffic and workload demands. We will discuss the differences between **horizontal** and **vertical scaling**, explore how to scale microservices efficiently using **Kubernetes** and **AWS**, and provide a **real-world example** of scaling a **Java-based microservice** on **AWS**.

Horizontal vs. Vertical Scaling

1. Horizontal Scaling (Scaling Out): Horizontal scaling, or **scaling out**, involves adding more instances of a service or application to distribute the load. Each new instance is typically a clone of the existing one, and they work in parallel to handle requests.

Advantages of Horizontal Scaling:

- **Improved Fault Tolerance:** If one instance fails, others can continue serving requests, ensuring high availability.

266

- **Better Load Distribution:** By distributing traffic across multiple instances, horizontal scaling can handle a higher volume of requests more efficiently.
- **Scalable by Design:** Horizontal scaling allows for seamless scaling as traffic grows. New instances can be added as needed without affecting the performance of the existing system.

Example: For a microservice that processes user registrations, you could have multiple instances of the service running behind a **load balancer**. If the traffic increases, additional instances can be added to distribute the load evenly.

2. Vertical Scaling (Scaling Up): Vertical scaling, or **scaling up**, involves increasing the resources (CPU, memory, storage) of a single server or instance. This method upgrades the hardware or resource allocation of the existing instance to handle more requests.

Advantages of Vertical Scaling:

- **Simplicity:** Vertical scaling is often easier to implement, as it involves upgrading existing infrastructure rather than adding new instances.
- **Reduced Complexity:** In some cases, scaling up avoids the complexity of managing multiple instances and services.

Disadvantages of Vertical Scaling:

- **Limits to Scaling:** There's a limit to how much you can scale up a single server. Eventually, you will hit resource constraints, and scaling vertically may not be sufficient.
- **Single Point of Failure:** Scaling vertically on a single instance can create a risk if the instance goes down.

Example: For a service that processes large datasets, you might scale vertically by increasing the memory or CPU of the instance running the service. However, this approach is limited by the capacity of the server hardware.

How to Scale Microservices Efficiently with Kubernetes and AWS

1. Scaling with Kubernetes:

Kubernetes is a powerful platform for managing containerized applications and is widely used for **scaling microservices** in production environments. Kubernetes makes it easy to horizontally scale services by adjusting the number of replicas of a given pod.

- **Horizontal Pod Autoscaling (HPA):** Kubernetes can automatically scale the number of replicas of a pod based on resource usage metrics such as **CPU utilization** or **memory usage**. The Horizontal Pod Autoscaler (HPA) automatically adjusts the number of replicas to meet demand.

Configuring HPA in Kubernetes: Here's an example of how to configure HPA for a **ProductService** running in Kubernetes.

1. **Create a deployment for ProductService**:

yaml

```yaml
apiVersion: apps/v1
kind: Deployment
metadata:
  name: product-service
spec:
  replicas: 3
  selector:
    matchLabels:
      app: product-service
  template:
    metadata:
      labels:
        app: product-service
    spec:
      containers:
        - name: product-service
          image: product-service:latest
          ports:
            - containerPort: 8080
```

269

2. **Configure Horizontal Pod Autoscaler**:

yaml

```yaml
apiVersion: autoscaling/v2beta2
kind: HorizontalPodAutoscaler
metadata:
  name: product-service-hpa
spec:
  scaleTargetRef:
    apiVersion: apps/v1
    kind: Deployment
    name: product-service
  minReplicas: 3
  maxReplicas: 10
  metrics:
    - type: Resource
      resource:
        name: cpu
        target:
          type: Utilization
          averageUtilization: 50
```

In this example:

- The `product-service` deployment starts with 3 replicas.

- The HPA scales the number of pods between 3 and 10 based on CPU utilization, with the target average CPU usage set to 50%.

2. Scaling with AWS:

AWS offers various services and tools to scale microservices efficiently, including **Amazon EC2**, **Elastic Load Balancing (ELB)**, **Amazon ECS**, and **Amazon EKS**. Here, we'll focus on scaling microservices using **Amazon EC2** and **Elastic Load Balancer (ELB)** for horizontal scaling.

- **Elastic Load Balancer (ELB)**: ELB automatically distributes incoming application traffic across multiple EC2 instances to ensure no single instance is overloaded.
- **Auto Scaling Groups**: EC2 instances can be managed by **Auto Scaling Groups**, which automatically adjust the number of instances based on demand.

Setting Up Auto Scaling with EC2:

1. **Launch EC2 Instances**: Create EC2 instances running your Java-based microservices.
2. **Create an Auto Scaling Group**: Define the minimum, maximum, and desired number of instances based on the expected load.
3. **Configure the Load Balancer**: Use **AWS ELB** to distribute traffic to your EC2 instances. The ELB will

automatically route incoming requests to healthy instances.

Example of an **Auto Scaling Group** configuration:

json

```
{
    "AutoScalingGroupName": "ProductServiceASG",
    "LaunchConfigurationName":
"ProductServiceConfig",
    "MinSize": 3,
    "MaxSize": 10,
    "DesiredCapacity": 5,
    "AvailabilityZones":    ["us-east-1a",    "us-
east-1b"]
}
```

In this example:

- The **Auto Scaling Group** ensures that between 3 and 10 instances of **ProductService** are running, based on traffic demand.

3. Using Amazon ECS or EKS for Containerized Microservices: If you are using containers to deploy microservices, **Amazon ECS (Elastic Container Service)** or **Amazon EKS (Elastic Kubernetes Service)** are excellent tools for managing containerized microservices at scale.

- **ECS** allows you to manage the scaling of containers with services and tasks.
- **EKS** provides a fully managed Kubernetes service, allowing you to take advantage of Kubernetes' scaling features (like **Horizontal Pod Autoscaler**).

Example: Scaling a Java Microservice on AWS

Let's walk through a practical example of scaling a **Java-based microservice** running on **Amazon EC2** and managed by **Auto Scaling Groups**.

1. Create EC2 Instances for the Product Service:

Assume that the **ProductService** is a Java-based microservice that handles product data. You first create an EC2 instance and install the **ProductService** application on it.

2. Configure Auto Scaling:

You then configure an **Auto Scaling Group** to automatically adjust the number of EC2 instances based on traffic. The Auto Scaling Group can scale the **ProductService** between 3 and 10 instances, depending on demand.

3. Set Up Elastic Load Balancer (ELB):

An **Elastic Load Balancer** distributes traffic to the instances of **ProductService**. It monitors the health of instances and ensures that traffic is only routed to healthy instances.

- Configure the ELB to forward requests to port 8080 (the port on which the ProductService is running).

4. Set Up CloudWatch Monitoring:

Use **Amazon CloudWatch** to monitor the performance and health of your EC2 instances, including CPU utilization, memory usage, and network traffic. You can create **CloudWatch Alarms** that trigger Auto Scaling actions if certain thresholds are met (e.g., CPU usage exceeds 80%).

Summary

In this chapter, we covered essential techniques for **scaling microservices** to handle high traffic loads:

- We discussed **horizontal scaling (scaling out)** and **vertical scaling (scaling up)**, highlighting the benefits of scaling out with multiple instances in a distributed system.
- We explored how to scale microservices using **Kubernetes** with **Horizontal Pod Autoscaling (HPA)**

274

and how to scale microservices on **AWS** using **Auto Scaling Groups** and **Elastic Load Balancer (ELB)**.

- We provided a **real-world example** of scaling a Java-based **ProductService** on AWS, including the use of **EC2 instances**, **Auto Scaling**, **ELB**, and **CloudWatch** for monitoring and scaling based on demand.

By applying these scaling strategies, you can ensure that your microservices architecture is both **highly available** and **cost-effective**, able to handle growing traffic while maintaining optimal performance. In the next chapters, we will continue to explore **advanced scaling techniques** and best practices for **distributed systems**.